D0771441

Golden
Words

Golden Words

The
A *to* Z TOOLKIT
for
CHANGING YOUR LIFE
ONE WORD *at a* TIME

SALLY STONE, ED.D

wisdom
heart

WISDOM HEART, LLC

Published by Wisdom Heart, LLC © 2015 by Sally Stone

All rights reserved. No part of this book may be reproduced in any form or by any electronic or mechanical means, including information storage and retrieval systems, without permission in writing from the author. For information, contact Sally Stone at www.DrSallyStone.com.

The content of this book is for general instruction only. Each person's physical, mental, emotional, and spiritual condition is unique. The instruction in this book is not intended to replace or interrupt the reader's relationship with a physician or other professional. Please consult your doctor for matters pertaining to your specific health and diet.

Printed in the United States of America

ISBN: 978-0-9969159-0-8 (paperback)
ISBN: 978-0-9969159-1-5 (ebook)

BODY, MIND & SPIRIT / Inspiration & Personal Growth
BODY, MIND & SPIRIT / Mindfulness & Meditation
PSYCHOLOGY / Hypnotism

Cover design by Laura Duffy
Book design by Karen Minster
Cover concept by Sally Stone
Word cloud art by Sally Stone

This book is dedicated to my mom and dad,

who gave me life and love,

to my stepdad, Bob,

who nourished me with words,

and to all the celestial and earth angels

who've inspired me to

stay the course on my journey.

Who is the most nurturing person you know?
Talk to yourself like that.

ELENA KAISER

Contents

PART ONE

THE INTERACTIVE DICTIONARY TOOLKIT
Golden Words You Can Use

PART TWO

THE SCIENCE OF GOLDEN WORDS, MANTRAS, AND HYPNOSIS

Author's Note

A book about golden words wouldn't be complete without addressing the flashes of spiritual insight that lie at the pinnacle of positive human experience. Since I refer to these types of experiences throughout this book, I'd like to share how I've used those terms.

I believe the spiritual happiness we seek is our true nature, which is identified in meditation traditions as the Higher Self or simply the Self. The state of our Higher Self is love, peace, joy, bliss, freedom, purity, clarity, connectedness, light, and wholeness. No matter what we experience in life—ups or downs, health or disease, community or solitude, poverty or wealth—the Higher Self remains united with the nature of the universe. Various methods help us stabilize ourselves in the experience of the Higher Self. Golden words are one of the vehicles for living happily in this world and guiding us to those higher states.

In spiritual traditions, the universal energy goes by many names including God, Spirit, Divine Mind, Cosmic Consciousness, Cosmic Mind, Great Spirit, Universal Design, Brahman, the Tao, Allah, All That Is, the Absolute, the Truth, Infinite Consciousness, and others. In truth, the ineffable experience of Spirit usually leaves us wide-eyed with joy, but groping for words. Poetry steps in when words fall short to describe the deep, oceanic experience of infinity that overwhelms the rational mind.

Throughout this book, I've used a variety of terms interchangeably to express this poetic experience of universal energy, but if you have a word or words you're more comfortable with, please make a substitution as you read.

If you'd like to see additional golden words in future editions of this book, please send me a note that includes your reasons for including them. I'd enjoy discussing your suggestions as well as your favorite golden words and tools.

Best wishes,
Sally

The Living Power of Words

———

*It is better to conquer yourself than to win
a thousand battles. Then the victory is yours.
It cannot be taken from you, not by angels
or by demons, not by heaven or by hell.*

BUDDHA

How do you speak to yourself throughout the day? Are you an architect of despair or a cheerleader of your own victory? Do you shrug your shoulders and wonder if any of it really matters, or do you guide yourself through challenges, calling on your intuition and trustworthy resources? How do you experience the words you say to yourself and hear from others? Do you feed yourself unhealthy words that cast shadows on you and your life, or do you nourish yourself with positive words?

I began learning techniques for mantra repetition, affirmations, and positive thinking in the mid 1980s. I believed these practices would help me lead a happier life, so I diligently practiced them—despite feeling skeptical about some of their effects. Certain aspects of my life, especially my career, unfolded magically and encouraged me to follow my intuition. In other areas, in particular relationships both personal and professional, my efforts sometimes ended in disappointment. These mixed experiences made me wonder if I should be disillusioned with myself or with positive thinking.

I kept my cynicism at arm's length, hidden from others, and dove deeper into meditation. Meditation offered insights, growing levels of awareness, and access to an independent source of happiness that offset my disappointments— it felt good. As for the parts of my life that weren't going so well, I distracted myself by keeping busy at work, at the gym, and with my friends. I enjoyed the life I'd created, and did my best to practice gracious acceptance by modifying some of my dreams and letting go of others.

Over the years, I built a successful career, eventually earning a doctoral degree in education, two teaching awards, and a wide variety of professional opportunities. I was in excellent physical condition thanks to hours spent at the gym and an organic, plant-based diet. But I had given up on finding a partner (one relationship had ended in violence), lost two children before they were born, and walked away from a number of youthful dreams, including working in complementary medicine, writing, and using intuition as a guide in *all* areas of my life.

I partitioned my life into what worked and what didn't. I loved working with children, especially in the areas of expertise I'd developed, which were process writing and interest-oriented, inquiry-based curriculum. At work, I enjoyed children's curious minds, honest emotions, and unique needs, which made the outside world disappear. I dove into work, where I felt blessed to be paid for a labor of love and in sync with my intuition and creativity. I continued to ignore other aspects of my life believing the sacrifices I'd made and the challenges, traumas, and disappointments I'd experienced were normal.

As the years went by, close friends and mentors urged me to pursue other activities, both professional and personal. One of them suggested, "You help all the children birth their dreams and talents. You should give some of your own a chance." These words struck a chord deep in my psyche and sparked many research, curriculum, and publication projects. But there was only so much I could juggle, and I didn't know how to change a successful career midstream. I dismissed that notion as impractical and unwise, especially financially. I had built a fortress of security and planned to stay there.

Then, I was severely injured in a bicycle accident. Through the unlikely combination of an ecstatic, near-death experience and the grueling pain and long-winded healing journey that followed, I began to understand the living power of words and how I could use them to forge a more balanced, happier life.

The Accident:
Meeting Angels and Ancestors

Four days before the accident, I had a dream that turned out to be prophetic. It was less a warning than a glimpse into the inevitable. My dream had four scenes.

> First, I felt wet blood on my hand. The blood stood out against a dim, black and white scene. Next, I was lying in bed listening to screaming-loud rock music. The noise was so irritating to my nervous system, I felt like I'd been put through a shredder. Next to my bed I noticed a black box with a sliding volume control switch. When I slid the switch to zero, I was suddenly wrapped in complete silence, an invisible cocoon of sweet healing. In the last scene, I set the timer on a treadmill for 35 minutes. When I began to jog, and realized I could move and use both my arms, I was flooded with ecstasy and gratitude. Smiling, I raised my arms in victory.

I lay in bed with my eyes closed, drifting in the space between waking and sleeping so I could remember the dream. The blood felt real. Was it mine? What had happened to my nervous system? The silence had a healing texture and sensation, like loving hands. The ecstasy of jogging puzzled me because I liked to run, but it didn't flood me with gratitude. And my arms and hands worked just fine. At the time, I worked out for about 15 hours a week and thought I was invincible. A victory celebration for running 35 minutes on the treadmill seemed extreme, not to mention silly.

By the time I set out on my bicycle on the day of my accident, I'd forgotten about the dream. I was mourning my dad, who three weeks earlier had been suddenly incapacitated by a stroke that robbed him of speech and mobility. Our relationship had always been difficult, with each of us struggling for control, but I always thought there'd be time to sort through those issues. Now it seemed impossible.

Throughout my life, I'd made many sacrifices to win his approval, but these decisions had always left me feeling conflicted and empty. Now that he couldn't speak, I wondered if I'd ever resolve my feelings. I planned to visit him later that day, when I felt more balanced, and decided to clear my head by taking a bike ride.

The weather was unseasonably warm for a Midwestern March—about 80° F. So I put on my khaki shorts and a black sports bra, which showed off my six-pack abs, before heading out. Pushing on the pedals and feeling the fresh air on my face was a welcome relief from standing around the hospital wishing my dad would recover. I headed for a trail that would take me through the woods and up to the beach, where I planned to sit by the water and let the waves wash away my grief. I would stare at my favorite shades of blue—in the sky and the water—and let their soothing colors relax my mind. My perspective and sense of wholeness would be restored for a little while.

I rode through town on the sidewalk, then came to a four-lane highway, where I rode along the sidewalk for about a half-mile. Cars buzzed by on my left, but the woods on my right fueled my anticipation of the trail ahead. I pedaled up the hilly sidewalk, then flew downhill to the stoplight. Gliding down I felt carefree, forgetting my heavy heart and obligations for a few moments. I crossed another four-lane highway and pedaled up the bridge over the expressway, which I had to cross to reach the trail. On the other side of the highway, I'd get my quiet time in nature.

Up I went again, over the bridge, and downhill, pushing on the pedals for my next glide to freedom. But as I cruised down, it loomed before me: a construction site with no barriers to warn me of the gaping gravel pit where there used to be a sidewalk. Too late, and impossible to rewind, I had nowhere to go but down.

My Near-Death Experience: Forgiveness, Resolution, and Love

When I was a child, I experienced an interconnected energy that flowed through everything. It was this intuitive sense of God that led me to meditation, yoga, and prayer. But despite my experiences and beliefs, I was unprepared for the dramatic, dreamlike visions in my near-death experience. I honestly don't know if I was "clinically dead" for any length of time because I'd gone out riding alone. What transpired may have been an out-of-body experience. Either way, what happened next changed me forever.

> I hit the ground and lifted out of my body. At first I felt
> disoriented, then I saw my own crumpled body sprawled on the
> ground. I panicked, wondering if I was dead, but when I realized
> how light and peaceful I felt floating around, I surrendered to
> being out of my body. I noticed a golden thread connecting me to
> my body, then I shifted up to a panoramic awareness of the
> landscape. It was like standing in the center of a carousel, where
> everything around me was moving with energy, but I was in the
> center of stillness. The trees glowed with light and pulsed with

life energy. Their branches and leaves showered me with ecstatic, unconditional love. The surrounding forest was like a lighthouse of energy breathing in a slow, rhythmic pulsation of love. This energetic pulsation was the underlying matrix of the universe, alive and breathing. Whoosh... Whoosh... Whoosh...

The space near me filled with soft light, a path of cotton-ball clouds forming an entryway to another plane of existence. A short gray guide appeared, and I floated with him along this path to where my beloved grandmother, grandfather, and preschool teacher were standing near the two children I'd lost before they were born. Farther away, I saw my other grandmother, who'd been unkind at times. She kept her distance, but smiled. When my awareness connected with her, she communicated to me without speaking. We exchanged blocks of ideas and feelings all at once.

I remembered the challenges of our relationship when she was alive, but I felt something different now. I sensed she'd been a protective force since her passing, watching over me in ways she hadn't done during her life. In fact, it dawned on me that my career had been stable ever since her death. I somehow knew she'd been helping me, which brought forgiveness and resolution to our relationship. A weight fell away.

My awareness shifted to the others. I dearly missed my grandfather, who'd died when I was three, and took solace in the few memories of us together. I didn't have any living children, and at times felt unbearable grief for the loss of these two before they were born. Now I was with them and felt myself as their mother, which gave me a sense of completion. I also sensed that my grandparents and preschool teacher were taking care of them, which set me at ease.

The spirits of my children, who I'd intuited as a boy and a girl, began dancing around me in a joyful spiral while playing off-tune music. They sounded just like kids who are learning to play instruments, which made me laugh. They washed away my grief with their carefree joy and playfulness. They communicated that I should honor the miracle of life, which I'd felt inside myself when I'd been pregnant. That miracle of life was the healing force. They coaxed me to be happy and play like a child. Our meeting brought deep comfort and peace. Another resolution.

I left the ancestral plane along the cotton-ball path with my gray guide, then came to a swirling portal of bright light. The portal hummed with the same rhythm, its whirling energy breathing in and out. I shifted through it to a place where the atmosphere was like a tangible substance radiating light, yet I couldn't touch it.

I met a being of glowing light. She seemed to be clothed in shimmering woven light, yet her glow came from within. She radiated pure love and kindness, untainted by the earthly doubt and cynicism I carried in myself.

As she came closer, I experienced a tangible silence. Stillness replaced the sensation of flying; bliss and freedom came to a standstill. I no longer had any internal motivations, but felt completely receptive and at the same time lacked expectation. Time was past, present, and future simultaneously. In the compression of time into all-at-once, everything had already been completed. There was nothing more to be, to do, or to have. Contentment replaced ambition. I was done, complete, and whole.

Space itself was infinite, as was each particle of space, imbuing this plane of existence with what I could only call

God, on both a macro and micro level. In this infinite space, where linear time was One and All-Pervasive, I didn't want or need anything, but simply existed as a complete spiritual being. Just a sliver of my awareness still sensed my body.

I knew I didn't belong there, but I wanted to stay. I projected this desire to the Light Being.

She responded, "No," without voice.

Disappointed, I prepared myself to go back, but then this Light Being gave me the understanding that I had to go back for love.

Leave this place of love and go back for love? I thought about my life challenges. Always busy, never catching up. I'd used constant activity at work and in the gym to shield myself from looking at the parts of my life that weren't working. I had many joys in my life, but carried inside myself a struggle for survival, unprocessed grief, and gnawing resentments.

"My life is difficult. And now my body is broken," I thought.

She responded, "You'll find healing and love. Reclaim your innocence and experience compassion in the face of every facet of human nature. Experience the pure love of angels, eyes wide open, in light of terrible grief and profound joy. This is the wise innocence of unconditional love."

"How?" I wondered. I sensed my own skepticism and disbelief underneath this perfect contentment.

She drew my attention to a flock of light orbs, which I sensed were angels. These angel-orbs each radiated positive feelings: love, joy, whimsy, playfulness, abundance, wonder, contentment, connection, tenderness, trust, compassion, wisdom, strength, courage, loyalty, celebration, freedom, lightheartedness, and unconditional support. These feelings were present all at once, though I could sense them separately, like listening for the individual notes of each instrument in a full orchestra.

"They're here to help. Just ask," the Light Being told me.

The chorus of angel-orbs with their positive feelings drew closer and brushed against me, giving me the experience of positive possibilities: abundance, love, joy, laughter, whimsy, trust, freedom, and even good-natured, playful mischief filled me with optimism and delight.

Then the Light Being came closer and joined with my consciousness. In that Oneness, the doubting, small parts of me were erased the way light erases darkness. What remained was a state of being without judgment, worry, or doubt. When we separated, I could still feel her state, but also my own, which had changed. In place of cynicism and doubt, I felt faith in living a life that's worthy of the state of angels—a life that inspires trust that angels, guides, and ancestors watch over us, trust in the human heart to be good, and compassion for human struggles, losses, and mistakes. This feeling solidified into an unshakeable pillar of strength and purpose. I knew without question that the purpose of human existence was to awaken our own better nature and invite angels to help us.

With these glimpses into a promising future, I was ready to follow the golden thread back to my body. Instead, another portal opened up, this time to a darker space. A white winged horse, like the mythological Pegasus, beat a rhythm to the same underlying pulsation of the universe itself. The wingbeats drew us through a dark tunnel that opened to a velvety black sky full of stars.

The landscape was covered in misty tributaries of energy pools. Tall thin monks with long brown robes tied at the waist walked near the streams carrying lanterns and staffs. I knew this was a wishing place. The energy in these pools was the substance from which things are born. Wish upon a star and pure energy forms itself according to your desire. There's no need to really wish on a star, but I somehow knew that long ago others who traveled to this place of stars and energy pools had created that mythology.

I felt ambivalent about wishing. I'd enjoyed the sense of magic but hadn't reconciled the challenges. Perhaps wishing was nothing more than putting on rose-colored glasses to soften an uncertain future. Then there was Dad. I'd wanted his support and been disappointed, but I hung onto blame instead of taking responsibility for my own creations. In all this blaming, I'd lost touch with what I wanted. I held resentment in that place, like an emotional bookmark. This had clouded my heart with skepticism about love and life. I realized now it was up to me. What do I want? What should I want? Is it safe to have desires? Is it too late? What if I think I want something, then I don't? Is it okay to be powerful?

I understood from the guides here that if I wanted to learn to wish again I should play like a child and experiment like a mad scientist. If you bake a pie and it flops, just laugh and make another one. If the pie is delicious, enjoy it and share with others. Energy takes form based on desire and expectation, so trust and expect the best. Stretch your wings, fool around, and play for the joy of it.

What I saw most clearly was how I'd given up my power of wishing because I'd asked others to be the grantors of my wishes, and when they'd said no, I'd taken that to be the final answer. It never occurred to me that I'd given away my wishing power. Now it was time to let go of wishing that others would bring me fulfillment and reclaim my own creative power.

I remembered a series of wishes I'd made throughout my life. At age 6, I wanted to be a pianist; at 8, a writer. From ages 13 to 19, I wanted to be a naturopath, and when I was in college I toyed with nature photography. There had been pressure on me to become a concert pianist, but I didn't want to perform, so my lessons were stopped. My other interests were considered impractical, unconventional, and expensive.

I came to believe that I shouldn't take a risk unless I knew it would turn out well. But who can know that in advance? Experimenting like a mad scientist with the interests that brought me joy was the only way to see what might happen. What I most wanted was to engage in something just for the joy of it. Then I laughed because I realized that even when I thought I'd abandoned my interests, they followed me in one form or another and brought me joy.

What I'd perceived as blocks in my path, which I thought had robbed me of what I wanted, had actually put me in the right place, at the right time, with the right people. I wanted to hang onto the anger about those blocks and the people I thought had created them, but gratitude began trickling into that place. Everything was in sync. The pattern of my life made sense.

I also realized that whatever I needed had always been provided. Sometimes we earn those things and other times people offer us gifts. There are infinite possibilities for the way in which what we need comes into existence. My worries disappeared into trust and contentment.

The beings in long robes with lanterns were teachers of creating something out of what appeared to be nothing, but the energy around them was not nothing. This matrix was modeling clay that could be formed into anything. Completely free of judgment, something could be created instantly with intention.

When our judgment, doubt, or other emotions clouded an intention, the wish changed into something unintended, and sometimes unwanted. Learning to be free of judgment and selfish desires made energy available for pure, positive creating.

Not all wishes come true. Sometimes there are lessons and patterns that can't be undone by wishing, yet wishing sets into motion what needs to be done or learned to attain or resolve the wish. Because of this, we have little control over the timeline or form that our wish takes. However, just as attention determines our direction, our emotional focus may eventually pull the wish into our physical lives in one form or another.

When these insights were complete, I returned through the tunnel. I felt the angel-orbs' positive energy and saw my Light Being once again. Then I reconnected in the carousel of nature. I felt reluctant. Death was not bad. Death was easy and full of delights. The accident had been surprising, but slipping out of my body had been easy. Now it was okay to return, despite the challenges of life. The touch of this Light Being inspired me to love with wise innocence and feel compassion without cynicism. I would cherish the gifts from my ancestors and child-spirits, absorb the unconditional love of nature, experiment like a mad scientist, and work toward positive feelings with the help of the angel-orbs. I followed the golden thread until I slipped into my body.

When I came to, I noticed two hazy figures. I touched my cheek-bone, which was wet with blood and swollen up like an egg. *The wet blood and dim, misty setting was the first scene from my dream.* "Don't try to move," one figure told me gently.

I lapsed in and out of consciousness waking up once in the ambulance and again at that hospital. Scans were performed, my face and lips were stitched up and my fully abraded shoulder bandaged, before my mom drove me to the pharmacy for meds, then to her house for dinner. Looking in the hallway mirror at my face, I was shocked to see that the left side of my face was black and blue down to my neck and my bloody eye was swollen shut. By the next day, my whole face was black and blue to my collarbones. I'd had a concussion, but it wasn't deemed bad enough to stay in the hospital. Even though I'd seen blood, I was certain I'd be okay, jogging on that treadmill very soon.

But my recovery didn't proceed normally. I developed chronic pain, headaches, sensory sensitivities, chemical and food sensitivities, and a dysregulated immune system. For the next 22 months I worked with conventional doctors, but traditional treatment—medications combined with physical therapy—didn't heal me. I developed sound sensitivities that made normal sound feel like screaming-loud rock music. My nervous system felt shredded. *The second image from my dream had come true.*

I used all of my inner resources to continue my career as a university professor and educational coach, while spending the rest of my time working with specialists or resting quietly in solitude. I crawled into the silence I'd dreamed about, using the long periods of introspection to review my life, digest my near-death experience, and discover what made me feel better and what made me feel worse.

With so many doctors shrugging their shoulders at my situation, I felt a loss of control over my health. Regular exercise and yoga were impossible. All the other enjoyable and menial aspects of life I'd taken for granted only increased the pain.

Even meditation became difficult. I'd lie there repeating my mantra, my restless mind struggling with physical pain and life challenges. "Now what?" I wondered. I *knew* I was going to be okay, but I didn't know how, or how long it would take. Now I understood why I'd feel so grateful to run for 35 minutes on a treadmill again—because from where I sat, I couldn't even take a walk. One doctor even told me that people like me ended up in a wheelchair using a morphine pump to manage the pain. It was only my prophetic dream that gave me the certainty to know that wasn't my fate.

One day during my silent retreat into prayer, breathing, and contemplation of positive feelings, I recalled something my meditation teacher once said: "If you're going to think, think well of yourself. Think positive thoughts. I am worthy, I am beautiful, I am good." This, I realized, was one of the few things that was still completely under my control: *my self-talk.*

I thought about the feelings of the angel-orbs I'd been in contact with at the time of the accident and began to observe more closely how the words I used all day long to describe how I felt, what I needed to do, and how I would manage had either a medicinal effect or a destructive effect on my degree of comfort. I realized I had to focus completely on cultivating those positive states. This required a lot of self-effort at times.

Soon after, a medical acquaintance suggested I look into hypnosis. He said that hypnosis could have extraordinary healing benefits when practiced with an open mind and suggested specific research for me to read. I was so impressed with the research that I went a few steps further. Within a five-year period I became a certified hypnotist, a certified Integrative Nutrition health coach, and a Family Constellations facilitator. In the long stretches of solitude, I learned to dive deeper into my own intuitive wisdom, and use these skills for navigating positive language, food, healthy living, and family patterns. Immersing myself in this flow felt like coming home. Day by day, I took control of my self-talk and my own healing process.

Taking control of my self-talk was the beginning of a slow walk toward liberation from self-judgment. It also brought deep comfort to my physical body and offered much-needed peace of mind. Engaging in management of my self-talk demonstrated the power I had to bring myself joy or harm. We can't control how other people talk to us, we can't always control how our life proceeds, but we can learn to be kind to ourselves as we navigate all the ups and downs.

I also traveled for treatments to work with two unconventional doctors whose technology resolved the physical pain. At 22 months into my recovery, I worked with Donald Rhodes in Corpus Christi, Texas, who invented an electro-acupuncture machine that uses beat frequencies delivered through electrodes onto acupuncture and acupressure points. Using this machine, now called VECTTOR, enabled me to walk in nature again, keeping my pace slow as a turtle and my distance short. On my first walk, at the Corpus Christi Botanical Gardens, tears of gratitude streamed down my face as I enjoyed the bliss of nature. Soon after, I began carrying a camera to document the beauty of nature, which continued to inspire my healing efforts.

Within five years, I was taking long walks for hours on end, often with my camera gear. Then, following the advice of a trusted doctor, I traveled to New Orleans on the sixth anniversary of my accident, where I lived for 12 weeks while undergoing hyperbaric oxygen (HBOT) treatments with Paul Harch, a pioneer in the use of HBOT for concussions. These treatments resolved the pain. By year seven, I jogged on a treadmill, as well as outside, though I'd come to prefer long walks in nature.

As part of my healing contract with myself, I filled my life with activities I loved and learned to make better boundaries. I learned nature photography, continued to work at capturing the inspiring energy of nature's flow, and began to win awards for some of my photos. Finally, due to chemical sensitivities, the last artifact of my accident, I was forced to take early retirement. I'd hoped to work until full retirement age, but one of the specialists I worked with told me I wouldn't survive to see retirement age unless I removed myself from the chemical exposures I experienced on a regular basis in my workplace.

As soon as I retired from my full-time job, I dedicated myself to my private practice and began writing with the intent to communicate the importance of believing in ourselves, following our intuitive wisdom, and the reality of a spiritual dimension underlying our existence. Honestly, my intellectual, rational mind never imagined writing about life-changing meetings with angels, ancestors, and guides. It wasn't as if I didn't believe in those things, but as a person who believes in science and worked for over two decades in a traditional institution as a public servant, it wasn't something I felt comfortable speaking about freely. The fact is there are many ways of knowing, including the spiritual and the scientific. But sometimes it takes a dramatic experience to shake someone out of their skepticism not only about a spiritual reality, but also toward themselves.

A month before my father's death, I attended his 83rd birthday party. He sat propped up in his wheelchair, head tilted to one side, the stroke side of his face slightly fallen. I sat next to him so I could share some wildlife photos I'd taken. He stared intently at the computer screen as I talked about each photo.

When I finished, I closed the lid on my laptop and looked into his eyes. He gazed back at me and we beamed smiles at each other. Our gaze held for so long, two women on the sofa elbowed each other and pointed. Then everything disappeared except an ancient love that had been lost in years of anger, resentment, guilt, fear, and shame. This healing moment with my dad, where no speech was needed, showed me that doing what I loved and sharing it with love was the best way to find love. The people-pleasing and self-sacrifice I had relied on in the past hadn't brought me any closer to deepening positive relationships with him or any other people I cared about.

When I began to see my own clients for hypnosis and health coaching, I asked them questions to learn about their own positive words and resources. As I listened to them talk about what they wanted to create most in their lives, their desires felt familiar. Some wanted to resolve sugar cravings, others wanted to relax or overcome sleeplessness. Many wanted to understand their life purpose, reclaim their voice, decide what to do about a health or relationship crisis, learn to play again, fully grieve a great loss, or explore their own near-death experience. Others needed the right words and movements to shift themselves out of an unproductive family pattern, gain foothold in a healthier place, and move forward in their lives and relationships.

No matter what their individual goals, universally the people I've worked with want to feel love, freedom, empowerment, joy, and peace. The coaching and hypnosis processes I learned and use with my clients allows us to access their own intuitive wisdom, which gives us the information we need to work together toward those individual and universal goals. Recognizing and exercising their own intuitive wisdom also offers people confidence to move forward when they leave my office.

As powerful positive words took root in my own life and private practice, I began to keep track of the ones my clients used in their sessions as well as my own favorites. After each session, I added words to the list and as it grew longer, I alphabetized it. Then I had another dream—this one revealed a prophecy that I could fulfill myself. I dreamed I was in a large library and made myself comfortable against a stack with a big dictionary full of positive words. I opened the book, paged through it, and when I woke up in the morning, I felt great from reading all those positive words while I'd been sleeping.

I pulled out my hardcover dictionary and randomly looked through it for positive words. I found words like joy, laughter, appreciation, comfort, friend, liberty, plenty, and many others. Each word sparked uplifting memories and possibilities that shifted my energy in a positive direction.

Reading and working with positive words created such a natural high that I decided to expand my list into a book with a dictionary and tools for navigating the living power of words. As I worked, I reflected on the positive ways these words had impacted my life. I wondered what possibilities might be in store if I could maintain my focus on their vibrations. I realized that these words were more than just positive. When I'd activated them in my life, they were golden.

Choosing Golden Words

As I progressed in this project, it became evident that I needed a method for choosing golden words. I included all the words that described the positive feelings I experienced on *the other side*. I included the words I'd learned from my clients, and I wondered what, in fact, makes a word *positive* or *golden* to people in general? I put on my research hat to consider this question. We're all connected through a universal desire to experience good health, love, freedom, connection, peace, kindness, inspiration, compassion, significance, and upliftment. These are the most obvious golden words, but they aren't the only kinds.

On the flipside of all these uplifting words are the so-called negative emotions, but golden words don't eliminate emotions. In fact, the only thing negative about our emotions is our judgment of them or the way we act on them. Any type of positive thinking that doesn't address the whole package of our human experience is going to fail. Positive thinking doesn't eliminate challenging life experiences either. What's happened can't be erased, but what we learn and how we manage it can be positive. In fact, to me, that was one of the keys to turning positive words into gold.

As my research continued, I discovered 10 types of golden words. (These categories are discussed in Part Two's "From Serene to Silly: What Makes a Word *Golden?*") Then I read the dictionary and chose the words I wanted to include. Reading them was like eating gourmet chocolates—but without the calories. They're sweet and bring many surprising and delicious nutrients without the guilt of indulgent food. When I had finished, I had collected over 2,000 golden words.

To help readers put these golden words to good use, I made the dictionary interactive to go a step beyond the typical book on the shelf. After all, putting positive words into action is what makes them golden in your life. With that in mind, Part One of this book is called "The Interactive Dictionary Toolkit: Golden Words You Can Use" because it's designed to give you many positive and productive ways to interact with the words. (For even more ideas, see "How to Use This Book.")

Part Two of this book shows you how to write effective mantras and affirmations (see "Eight Principles for Crafting Effective Mantras, Affirmations, and Autosuggestions") and use relaxation and self-hypnosis to support your goals (see "Ten Steps to Relaxation and Self-Hypnosis"). It also explains the science and myths about hypnosis (see "Hypnosis: Fact and Fiction"). If you're new to hypnosis and trance states, be sure to check out this section to learn about the powerful, positive aspects of hypnosis and liberate yourself from the cultural myths, most of which arise out of stage hypnosis and the media. The facts you'll learn in this chapter will free you to enjoy the powerful techniques of trance, which can enhance mood, health, confidence, effectiveness, intuitive flow, and more.

I'd like to close this preface with a personal story about the beloved dictionary I used to find the golden words in this book. When I was 17, my mom remarried. My stepdad, Bob, impacted my life in many positive ways, foremost as a guidance counselor of the heart and mind. He also knew I loved to write and acted as my editor. One day he presented me with a gift: *The American Heritage Dictionary of the English Language.*[1] He advised me to, "Learn as many words as you can. Keep this by your side when you read and write. Words have the power to express exactly what you want to say."

At the time, I wasn't so interested in positive words per se, but I kept this four-pound, 1,491-page dictionary by my side while I read, pausing at unfamiliar words, and taking the time, despite my teenage impatience, to look them up. Sometimes I opened the dictionary to a random page and read through pages of words just for fun so I could use them in conversation with Bob. Forty years later, I found myself with this book in my lap and opened it to the letter A. I could have used the Internet as my resource but, because words feel alive to me, I wanted to hold them in my hands.

Learning words kept me close to my stepdad when distance and, eventually, his death separated us. The cover from my dictionary has come loose from so much use, but like the main character in Margery Williams' *The Velveteen Rabbit*, some things only become real when they're old and falling apart. Just as the Velveteen Rabbit eventually became real to the little boy who owned him, the living quality of words becomes real when you start to pay attention. When I fell apart and had to put myself back together, a great many words and concepts became glue for my body, mind, and spirit. This is the living power of words, which is accessible to everyone.

Realizing that words are alive and have golden properties has been one of the many blessings of my bike accident. I've mourned many losses, but am blessed to be alive, have a home, friends, the physical health to exercise and walk in the beauty of nature, loving family support, and work that I love. Golden words and the tools and mentors that help me absorb them—angels, teachers, meditation, hypnosis, coaching, intuition, and nurturing self-care—provide a guiding light. With continued use, awareness of the power and life energy of words grows, and so does the desire to choose them carefully—for their effect can be profound. Once you know them, your knowledge can't be undone. I believe that golden words and the tools I've shared here can light your way, too.

Acknowledgments

I would like to thank my mother, who has celebrated my healing landmarks, both large and small, with effervescent optimism, and enthusiastically cheered on *Golden Words*. You personify golden words and have made your life circumstances into a golden life. As Bob always said, "You are a 'Rae' of sunshine." Thank you for your kindness, unconditional love, and support.

To Joy Putnam, my dear friend, and life coach, who inspired me to be vulnerable and reveal myself in these stories. To my "soul" sister, Maggie Smith, thank you for your valuable insights, which helped me shape this book. To Miranda B. Norris, thank you for your sense of humor, irony, and loving support. To my mentor and cheerleader, Elena Kaiser, for your unconditional support.

A special thank you to Sonia Choquette, my mentor and champion, for believing in me while I found my voice. During my grimmest healing days, your encouragement carried me through dark times and birthed two books. Because of you I know it's possible to live a wholly intuitive life in sync with Spirit.

To my dream team, Christina Verigan, editor; Karen Minster, interior book designer; Laura Duffy, cover designer; and Lindsay Galvin, proofreader. Thank you for being my shoemaker's elves and working your magic behind-the-scenes to make *Golden Words* into this book. Without each of you, I would still have a stack of papers on my office desk.

To all the meditation masters, teachers, and spiritual helpers who opened me up to the extraordinary universe of wonder in the inner realms, thank you with all my heart for guiding me to the riches that lie within. To my hypnosis mentors from The Wellness Institute (Laurie Rose, Renee Garrick, and Mark Roy) and the National Guild of Hypnotists™ (Linda Williamson, Karen Hand-Harper, and Larry Garrett), thank you for showing me how to empower and support myself and my clients with hypnosis.

To the authors whose research I drew from to write this book, thank you for your scholarship, inspiration, and encouragement.

To Dr. Dean Deng, Qigong Master and acupuncturist, who taught me the ancient practice of Qigong and "needled me" with positive chi in many forms while I wrote this book.

A heart full of thanks to Joshua Rosenthal, Founder of The Institute for Integrative Nutrition, Lindsey Smith, and the staff at IIN for your unflagging support.

A final outpouring of thanks to all my clients for opening your hearts and sharing your bright spirits with me as we grow and evolve together on this great adventure of experiencing and expressing the riches within.

To the angels and their golden vibrations, thank you for lifting me up, infusing me with hope, and sharing your unique gifts with me. To all the golden words who kept me company while I wrote this book, thank you for filling me with laughter, joy, vulnerability, grace, adventure, delight, awe, gratitude, light, peace, connection, clarity, balance, courage, curiosity, spirit, angels, friendship, love, service, humility, optimism, and countless blessings.

How to Use This Book

Part One: The Interactive Dictionary Toolkit

The workbook format of The Interactive Dictionary Toolkit invites you to use golden words and tools in a variety of ways. You can add your own words, mantras, and affirmations to customize the book and help you incorporate the words and tools into your daily life. If you don't want to write in the book, you can use a journal to interact with the words and tools.

You can also thumb through the dictionary when you need a boost. Reading golden words is like drinking sacred medicine. Open the book to any page and drink the nectar of love, comfort, awe, fearlessness, or any of the other 2,000+ words you might encounter. Find one that fits the moment perfectly and see where it takes you. Choose a golden word to start your day, lift you up in a challenging moment, or end your day before you go to sleep.

The notes below explain each part of the toolkit and provide additional guidance so you can read through the resources and decide what works best for you.

Creating New Habits

Each letter of the alphabet has six resources. Since there are 26 letters in the alphabet, the book has its own natural pace. Reading one letter a day and practicing the associated tool will give you a chance to learn a little about how each one can help you harness the power of golden words.

This book also lends itself to rereading and carrying with you to look through in waiting rooms and coffee shops, at the beach or pool, on an airplane or on vacation, or sitting on a park bench waiting for a friend. If you find a tool you want to cultivate into a new habit, it's best to practice daily until what you want to create becomes a natural part of you and your routine. I recommend taking 21 to 30 days to practice and incorporate a new habit.

Six Resources for Each Letter in the Interactive Dictionary Toolkit

RESOURCE 1: WORD LISTS FOR EACH LETTER

Each letter is introduced with a list of golden words and a word-cloud graphic for visual learners. If you disagree with one or more of my golden word choices, please feel free to cross those words out of your book. I want you to feel empowered to choose words that are golden and important to you.

RESOURCE 2: SPACE TO ADD YOUR OWN GOLDEN WORDS

There is space for you to add your own golden words, which may be idiosyncratic and important to you. If you think your word choices are universal and belong in this book, please contact me through my website (www.DrSallyStone.com). I'd enjoy learning your golden words and your rationale for adding them.

RESOURCE 3: DEFINITIONS

The definitions are brief summaries written in my own words, with the aim of helping you soak in the golden words' magic. As you read the definitions, you might find they include other golden words you like. Simply reading through the words and definitions, and letting your mind drift, can be a healing experience.

RESOURCE 4: A Collection of Your Favorite Golden Words

While you read the golden words and definitions, write down your favorites. You'll be able to draw from those words to create mantras and affirmations in Resource 5.

RESOURCE 5: Your Mantra or Affirmation Using Your Favorite Golden Words

Following each activity, you have space to write your own mantra or affirmation using your favorite golden words. Please refer to "Eight Principles for Crafting Effective Mantras, Affirmations, and Autosuggestions" in Part Two for guidelines, or experiment on your own.

RESOURCE 6: Tools for Experiencing the Transformative Power of Golden Words

I developed each tool based on the successful experiences of my hypnosis-health coaching clients, yoga students, education and training, and personal experiences. Some tools involve physical movement; others entail sitting or lying down quietly. I purposely included tools with various learning styles in mind. Some tools are designed to generate a spiritual experience, while others have practical applications, such as managing discomfort, dissipating food cravings, eliminating obstacles, navigating difficult situations, and others.

Most of the tools require an investment of 15–20 minutes of your time. Others are designed for you to incorporate into your daily, weekly, or monthly activities. Once you're familiar with each tool, you'll be able to use many of them on the go, in various life situations.

As you become familiar with the processes embedded in each tool, you'll be able to mix and match them as well. For example, the Contemplate Benevolence tool could easily be modified to create a contemplation incorporating peace, love, contentment, abundance, or other golden words. With the Soothing Silk Scarves tool you can substitute warm water, the fragrance of a favorite flower, colors, or feelings from memories in place of a scarf. Once you're familiar with the tools, you can use them with the golden words in this book as creatively as you like to suit your own personal tastes.

You'll get the most benefit from these tools when you have a few minutes to relax. Each one provides information on how to prepare yourself to get the most from that tool, including instructions that will guide you into a gentle trance. I also provide "Ten Steps to Relaxation and Self-Hypnosis" in Part Two, to help you go deeper. However, it isn't necessary to use the 10 steps to benefit from the tools. A relaxed state, where you take your time and pay attention to your thoughts and feelings, combined with the concepts in "Eight Principles for Crafting Effective Mantras, Affirmations, and Autosuggestions" will make the tools effective for you.

Please note: The golden words and tools in this book are designed to help you access your intuitive wisdom and empower you to make positive life changes. They are not intended to replace or interrupt your relationship with a physician or other medical professional. The activities are not replacements for hypnosis, coaching, or therapeutic sessions with the appropriate professional. Please consult your doctor for matters pertaining to your specific health, diet, and medical condition.

Part Two: The Science of Golden Words, Mantras, and Hypnosis

In Part Two, I provide your intellectual mind with evidence for understanding the power of golden words. Some of you may feel, know, or otherwise intuit the power of golden words without having to know the science. It's common sense for the most part: you know what makes you feel good and what makes you feel bad. Even if you can accept the magic without having to know why, understanding the reasons will satisfy the intellectual part of your brain.

In Part Two, I also discuss evidence-based principles that show you how you can refine your approach to using golden words and phrases. In addition to these principles, you'll learn principles for relaxation and self-hypnosis, which also support the effectiveness of golden words. The bonus is that relaxing, in and of itself, is a positive healthful state to cultivate.

I. From Serene to Silly: What Makes a Word *Golden*?

While researching golden words, I discovered 10 categories for identifying them. This chapter will walk you through the categories and show you how to recognize the roles different types of words play in our lives and experiences. Examining the relationships between words, the self, and the wider world enables you to better harness the power of golden words for yourself.

II. Eight Principles for Crafting Effective Mantras, Affirmations, and Autosuggestions

The words "mantra" and "affirmation" have come to be used and accepted in many contexts, from sacred to everyday, whereas the concept of auto-suggestion is less well-known. To clarify my use of these terms in this book, I've defined and used the concepts of mantras, affirmations, and autosuggestions to fit a wider, more encompassing application of positive, golden self-talk. The rest of this chapter is devoted to walking you through a process for creating positive change in your own life.

What would you like to change about your life? If you have something in mind when you read this chapter, you'll have a mantra or affirmation to use as an autosuggestion (positive self-talk) by the end of the chapter. If you have a list of several things you'd like to change, choose the one that's dearest to your heart. Once you've chosen your intention, read through the principles in order because they build on one another. They also work in concert, like the instruments in an orchestra, to make the change process work most harmoniously for you.

These eight principles will help you navigate the process in your own life, whether you're moving toward a large change or a small change. Understandably, some situations where you desire large changes are more complex than others and may require a support person or team to help you. Once you understand these principles, you'll be able to make better sense of who the supporters are in your life and how to choose them effectively.

This list of the eight principles gives a preview and an overview, which you can use as a checklist for managing your own process of positive change in your life. Have fun with it and celebrate your wins.

PRINCIPLE 1: Think big, but count the small changes

PRINCIPLE 2: Maintain the big picture in the present tense

PRINCIPLE 3: Create believable goals and adjust as needed

PRINCIPLE 4: Take advantage of habit, repetition, and emotion

PRINCIPLE 5: Mind your emotional tone

PRINCIPLE 6: Be affirmative

PRINCIPLE 7: Use "I statements"

PRINCIPLE 8: Keep a journal

III. Hypnosis: Fact and Fiction

As you read this chapter, sweep your mind clean of any myths you've learned about hypnosis so you can replace those fictions with science about its benefits, which come from the power of your own mind. Hypnosis can't make you do anything you don't want to do, though absurd images have been portrayed for entertainment. Hypnosis isn't magic, though it may seem to be if you've ever seen a stage hypnotist.

When a hypnotist works with people in private practice, the effects aren't magic either, though they may certainly seem to be at times. Rather, hypnosis is a natural process that employs the power of the mind to create beneficial changes in the way we feel mentally, physically, emotionally, and spiritually. Read this chapter to learn some of the science behind the magic in your own brain and body.

IV. Ten Steps to Relaxation and Self-Hypnosis

We're all very busy, so why should we bother to use valuable time for relaxation and self-hypnosis?

In our everyday states of mind, repeating golden words and phrases can be helpful, but I find where most people fall short in getting results comes from rushing through their autosuggestions. Positive, golden self-talk is more effective when you take the time to feel what you're saying or thinking as opposed to hurrying through to get it done. When you relax or use hypnosis, you slow down, become fully embodied, and can better state and *experience* your golden words and phrases with *feeling*. It's your embodied feeling that brings you the best results, not just saying the words.

Think of it this way: When you really engage with a book or television show, you experience what happens to the characters as if it were happening in real life. That's because you fall into a suggestible hypnotic state when you stare at a book or at the television screen without distractions. Your one-pointed focus blocks out peripheral disturbances, and your absorption in the story begins to feel real. We can take advantage of the suggestibility of the hypnotic state to give our own golden words and phrases a chance to feel more real as well. It's fun to watch TV and movies, but intentional self-hypnosis, where there's a chance to revise and believe in our own stories, will probably bring greater personal benefits.

PART ONE

INTERACTIVE DICTIONARY TOOLKIT

GOLDEN WORDS
YOU CAN USE

Abundant A

Abecedarian, Ability, Able, Abound, About-face, Abracadabra, Absolute, Absolve, Absorbed, Abundant, Accept, Acclaim, Accommodate, Accomplish, Accountable, Accurate, Ace, Achieve, Acknowledge, Action, Activate, Active, Acupuncture, Adapt, Add, Adept, Admirable, Admire, Adorable, Adore, Advantage, Adventure, Aesthetic, Affection, Affectionate, Affirm, Affirmation, Aficionado, Afterglow, Afterlife, Aganippe, Agape, Ageless, Agile, Agleam,

Agree, Agreeable, Ahimsa, Aid, Aim, Air, Ajna, Alacrity, Alchemy, Alert, Alight, Aliment, All-out, Allow, All Saints' Day, Ally, Alms, Aloha, Altruistic, Amaze, Ambition, Ambrosia, Amen, Amiable, Ample, Amuse, Anahata, Angel, Anger, Animated, Anthesis, Anticipate, Anticipation, Antidote, Appreciate, Aptitude, Archangel, Ardent, Armistice, Art, Artisan, Artist, Ascend, Asleep, Aspire, Assert, Assiduous, Assimilate, Assist, Assuage, Astonish, Astound, Astral, Astute, Athena, Athlete, Atman, Atonement, Attain, Attend, Attention, Attentive, Attract, Au Naturel, Aura, Aurora, Aurum, Auspice, Auspicious, Authentic, Author, Authority, Autograph, Autohypnosis, Autonomic, Autonomous, Autosuggestion, Autumn, Auxiliary, Avail, Avatar, Avocation, Awaken, Award, Awe, Awesome, Aye, Azure

ADD YOUR OWN GOLDEN **A** WORDS

_____

_____

_____

_____

_____

ABECEDARIAN: A person who teaches or studies the alphabet; a beginner or novice

ABILITY: The skill or talent to be able to do something

ABLE: Capable of doing something

ABOUND: Large in number

ABOUT-FACE: A reversal in attitude

ABRACADABRA: A magic word used to avert misfortune

ABSOLUTE: Perfect, complete

ABSOLVE: To clear of blame

ABSORBED: Engrossed, attentive

ABUNDANT: Plentiful, overflowing, full

ACCEPT: To receive gladly

ACCLAIM: Commendation, applause

ACCOMMODATE: To do a favor for

ACCOMPLISH: To succeed in something

ACCOUNTABLE: Responsible

ACCURATE: Correct

ACE: An expert; to do well

ACHIEVE: To accomplish successfully

ACKNOWLEDGE: To show recognition

ACTION: Movement

ACTIVATE: To initiate movement

ACTIVE: Busy, lively

ACUPUNCTURE: A therapeutic technique in traditional
Chinese medicine used to facilitate healing

ADAPT: To adjust to circumstances

ADD: To join together

ADEPT: Someone who has gained a high degree of expertise

ADMIRABLE: Worthy of respect and appreciation

ADMIRE: To look upon with respect and appreciation

ADORABLE: Lovable, charming

ADORE: To love deeply

ADVANTAGE: Favorable for success

ADVENTURE: An unusual journey or experience

AESTHETIC: A sense of beauty

AFFECTION: Tender feelings toward another person

Affectionate: Loving, caring

Affirm: Confirm, support, encourage

Affirmation: To declare something to be true

Aficionado: An enthusiastic admirer

Afterglow: The pleasant feeling after a good experience

Afterlife: Life after death

Aganippe: A spring on the legendary Mount Helicon that is sacred to the muses and provides inspiration

Agape: A state of wonder or amazement

Ageless: Eternal

Agile: Mentally alert

Agleam: Brightly shining

Agree: To give consent

Agreeable: Friendly, pleasant

Ahimsa: An Indian doctrine stating the sacredness of all life

Aid: Assistance

Aim: A goal, intention, or purpose

Air: What we breathe that allows us to live on Earth

Ajna: The third eye chakra, located between the eyebrows, corresponds to wisdom, clarity, intuition, and imagination

Alacrity: Eager willingness

Alchemy: The ability to transmute base metals into gold

Alert: Attentive, observant

Alight: Lit up

Aliment: Food, nourishment

All-out: Complete, without reservation

Allow: Permit

All Saints' Day: A November 1st festival in honor of saints

Ally: A friend

Alms: Charity given to the poor

Aloha: Love, affection; hello; farewell

ALTRUISTIC: Concerned for others; selfless, philanthropic

AMAZE: To fill with wonder

AMBITION: The desire to achieve

AMBROSIA: Nectar worthy of the gods

AMEN: Truly!

AMIABLE: Friendly

AMPLE: Abundant, bountiful

AMUSE: To charm or entertain

ANAHATA: The heart chakra, located in the center of the chest, corresponds to love, compassion, and acceptance

ANGEL: A spiritual being; a kind and lovable person

ANGER: Exasperation; annoyance

ANIMATED: Filled with excitement, spirited

ANTHESIS: The full bloom of a flower

ANTICIPATE: To see and act in advance; to look forward to something

ANTICIPATION: Expectation

ANTIDOTE: A remedy

APPRECIATE: To be thankful or grateful

APTITUDE: A natural skill or ability

ARCHANGEL: A celestial being whose position is above an angel

ARDENT: Expressing warmth

ARMISTICE: A truce

ART: A work of beauty with aesthetic value

ARTISAN: A skilled craftsperson

ARTIST: A person who creates works of art

ASCEND: Move upward

ASLEEP: Sleeping

ASPIRE: To strive toward a positive end

ASSERT: To express one's rights

Assiduous: Devoted, diligent

Assimilate: To absorb and incorporate knowledge

Assist: To give support

Assuage: To calm; to satisfy; to sweeten

Astonish: To feel with wonder, amazement

Astound: Astonish; fill with wonder

Astral: Pertaining to the stars

Astute: Perceptive in judgment; ingenious

Athena: The Greek goddess of wisdom and the arts

Athlete: A person with a natural ability for sports

Atman: The individual soul

Atonement: To make amends for an injury
or wrongdoing

Attain: To accomplish

Attend: To be present

Attention: Concentration upon something specific

Attentive: Considerate

Attract: To draw near; to be magnetic

Au Naturel: In a natural state

Aura: An invisible emanation of energy
or air about something

Aurora: A flashing, many-colored luminosity visible
in the polar/temperate regions

Aurum: The elemental gold

Auspice: A prophetic sign, especially from birds

Auspicious: Favorable circumstances; characterized by
good fortune, success

Authentic: Genuine

Author: One who creates a work of writing

Authority: The right and power to command

Autograph: A person's own signature

AUTOHYPNOSIS: The act of hypnotizing oneself

AUTONOMIC: Independent

AUTONOMOUS: Self-governing

AUTOSUGGESTION: The act of subconsciously accepting an idea
through repetition in order to change one's own behavior

AUTUMN: The season of the year when the weather cools,
the leaves turn colors and fall off the trees, and animals
begin to migrate or find places to hibernate for the winter

AUXILIARY: Giving additional support

AVAIL: Take advantage of an opportunity; to be of value

AVATAR: An exemplar; a deity in human or animal form

AVOCATION: An activity done for enjoyment outside
one's profession

AWAKEN: To become aware, awake, stir up interest

AWARD: A prize or recognition for quality or performance

AWE: Wonder, reverence inspired by something grand,
majestic, divine, sublime

AWESOME: Inspiring awe

AYE: Yes, affirmative

AZURE: Bright blue (this author's favorite color)

WRITE YOUR FAVORITE GOLDEN A WORDS HERE

_____

_____

_____

_____

_____

NOW USE YOUR FAVORITE GOLDEN **A** WORDS TO CREATE YOUR OWN MANTRA OR AFFIRMATION

Tool 1: Ready, Aim, Fire

Do you ever find yourself unfocused, with your attention wandering away from your goals? Take heart in the story of Arjuna, a great archer in the Indian epic *The Mahabharata,* who demonstrates the value of taking aim before letting your arrows fly.[1] This excellent advice applies to goals in general and the tools in the rest of this book.

Arjuna's fellow students were jealous because they perceived Arjuna, the great archer, to be the teacher's pet. Their teacher, Dronacharya, brought them together to dispel their resentment and illustrate how Arjuna had earned his admiration.

Dronacharya started by setting up a wooden target in the shape of a bird on a distant tree. He asked the warriors, one at a time, to take aim at the target with their bows and arrows and hit the eye of the bird. The first student up was Yudhishtra. After he took aim, Dronacharya stopped him and asked, "Yudhishtra, what do you see?"

Yudhishtra replied, "I see the bird, the tree, the fruit, and more birds."

Dronacharya told him not to fire his arrow. Next up was Duryodhana. After he took aim, Dronacharya stopped him, too, and asked the same question, "Duryodhana, what do you see?"

Duryodhana answered, "I also see the bird, the tree, leaves on the tree, the fruit, and other birds."

Dronacharya asked him not to fire his arrow either. Two more students drew their bows to fire their arrows, but Dronacharya stopped them, too, when they told him what they saw. Finally, it was Arjuna's turn. When Dronacharya asked Arjuna what he saw, Arjuna answered simply, "I see the eye of the bird."

"Fire," replied Dronacharya.

Arjuna's arrow pierced the bird's eye with complete accuracy, silencing his fellow students. Now his classmates understood why Arjuna was considered the best student. When you aim for something, everything else must disappear. Only then can the goal be attained.

I wish you all the best in reaching your goals using the principle from this story, the other tools and principles in this book, and helpers along the way who line up to support your goal.

Tool 2: The Art of Autosuggestion

As discussed in Part Two, an autosuggestion is a suggestion one makes to oneself. Since we talk to ourselves (silently or audibly) a great deal of the time, we're often giving ourselves autosuggestions. Therefore it's wise to think about what we say to ourselves and make that self-talk deliberate and positive.

Please read all the directions before proceeding.

1. Write Your Autosuggestion

The first step is to decide what you'd like to suggest to yourself. If you're not sure how to put your idea into words, please review the "Eight Principles for Crafting Effective Mantras, Affirmations, and Autosuggestions" from Part Two. If you're not sure what to focus on, flip through

The Interactive Dictionary Toolkit and see which words and ideas stand out to you. The words are here as a resource for just that reason. You can always start with Émile Coué's famous autosuggestion, "Every day, in every respect, I'm getting better and better," and see how that works for you. Coué's autosuggestion is general enough to be applied to many situations. You can also modify Coué's phrase to suit your own needs by changing the word "better" to happier, calmer, and so forth.

2. Relax

Find a place to lie down, like your bed, your yoga mat, or on a recliner. If you're concerned about getting too relaxed because you have an appointment, set a timer. If you do this before taking a nap or going to bed, then set your intention to fall into a deep sleep when you're done.

If you have time, use the "Ten Steps to Relaxation and Self-Hypnosis" in Part Two to bring yourself into a gentle trance. Please note that this isn't necessary, but would be helpful.

A quick way to relax is by taking a deep breath in and holding it for a few seconds. Allow your breath to flow through your whole body. Then let it go. Release any anxiety through your breath and let it float away. Repeat two more times. On the third breath, breathe in light of any color and let it flow through your body, allowing you to fall into a deep state of relaxation. Then close your eyes, and let your body sink into your bed, mat, or recliner, fully supported.

3. Repeat Your Autosuggestion

Slowly breathe in and out with each repetition as you use your fingers to keep count. Repeat your autosuggestion with feeling, as well as silently and slowly enough for confirming or opposing images, thoughts, or feelings to arise. Continue until you've repeated the autosuggestion 10 times, once for each finger. If you'd like to continue repeating the autosuggestion because you're receiving important insights and it feels good, please do so. If you drift off, that's alright. Just relax and breathe.

4. Come Back

Finally, come back from your experience slowly so you can remember the subtle images, ideas, and feelings that emerged for you. Write down each positive, affirming notion that arose. If negative ones came up, take note of how you plan to address them. For example, if you have a health issue and were able to see many ways you're improving, write that down. If you also saw all the ways you're still not well, write that down and reflect on what you're going to do about it. If you saw how your confidence is improving, write that down, and reflect on what changes that can bring.

5. Move On

Continue on with your day fueled by the insights and relaxation you acquired during your autosuggestion session—or go to sleep and sleep well.

NOTES

_____

_____

_____

_____

_____

Bountiful B

Babe, Baby, Balance, Balm, Barcarole, Bard, Bargain, Bask, Beach, Beatific, Beautiful, Beauty, Becalm, Bed of Roses, Befriend, Begin, Beginner, Believe, Belong, Beloved, Benediction, Benefactor, Beneficent, Beneficial, Benefit, Benefit of the Doubt, Benevolent, Benign, Bequeath, Best, Bestow, Best Seller, Bethink, Better, Bibliophile, Biographical, Birth, Bless, Blessing, Bliss, Bloom, Blossom, Blue Ribbon, Bodhisattva, Bold, Bonanza, Bonus,

Book, Born, Bountiful, Brainy, Brave, Brawn, Breath, Breathe, Breathtaking, Bright, Brilliant, Brio, Bubbly, Bud, Buoyant

ADD YOUR OWN GOLDEN B WORDS

_____

_____

_____

_____

_____

Babe: Baby or infant; an attractive woman; an innocent person

Baby: A very young child

Balance: A state of physical, mental, emotional, or spiritual equilibrium

Balm: A pleasant fragrance; a healing, soothing, comforting substance

Barcarole: The gondolier's song that has a rhythm that resembles the rowing of the gondolier

Bard: A singing poet, especially of the Celtic order

Bargain: An advantageous purchase

Bask: To enjoy something pleasant

Beach: The shore next to a body of water such as a lake, pond, or ocean

Beatific: Showing exalted joy or a blessed feeling

Beautiful: Pleasing to the senses, lovely

Beauty: A pleasing, lovely, or delightful quality

Becalm: To make still, soothe

Bed of Roses: Comfort, luxury

BEFRIEND: To aid, assist, act as a friend

BEGIN: To start something

BEGINNER: One who is beginning to learn something

BELIEVE: To have confidence that something is true

BELONG: To be part of something

BELOVED: One that is loved with great affection

BENEDICTION: A prayer for divine blessing

BENEFACTOR: One who offers aid

BENEFICENT: Characterized by acts of kindness

BENEFICIAL: Favorable, advantageous

BENEFIT: Something that enhances well-being

BENEFIT OF THE DOUBT: Offering a favorable ruling in
the absence of evidence

BENEVOLENT: A tendency toward good will, kind acts

BENIGN: Kind, gentle, mild

BEQUEATH: To pass down to someone, sometimes through a legal will

BEST: Excellent, superlative, great, surpassing others

BESTOW: To offer a gift or an honor

BEST SELLER: A book or other product that's sold in larger numbers
compared to others

BETHINK: To reflect

BETTER: Improved in quality

BIBLIOPHILE: Someone who loves books

BIOGRAPHICAL: Having to do with a person's life story

BIRTH: The beginning of life

BLESS: Confer well-being; bestow with talent

BLESSING: Good fortune

BLISS: Ecstatic, spiritual delight

BLOOM: To flower, blossom; prosper

BLOSSOM: Flourish

BLUE RIBBON: First prize, the highest honor or award

BODHISATTVA: An enlightened being who delays nirvana
   to assist others

BOLD: Courageous, fearless

BONANZA: A source of wealth such as a gold mine

BONUS: Jackpot, windfall, prize

BOOK: Printed pages joined together

BORN: Brought into existence

BOUNTIFUL: Generous, abundant, plentiful

BRAINY: Intelligent

BRAVE: Courageous

BRAWN: Well-developed muscle; physical strength

BREATH: The inhalation and exhalation of air by a living organism

BREATHE: To inhale and exhale

BREATHTAKING: Awe-inspiring

BRIGHT: Shining, brilliant light; intelligent; full of hope; cheerful

BRILLIANT: Bursting with light; vivid; glorious, splendid

BRIO: Vivacious

BUBBLY: Cheerful

BUD: The beginning of something

BUOYANT: Light-spirited

WRITE YOUR FAVORITE GOLDEN B WORDS HERE

NOW USE YOUR FAVORITE GOLDEN **B** WORDS
TO CREATE YOUR OWN MANTRA OR AFFIRMATION

_____

_____

_____

_____

_____

Tool: Contemplate Benevolence

Are you a worrywart? When you worry, where do you carry tension? Do your shoulders hunch up? Do you scrunch your forehead, clench your fists, or tighten your hips? Does your belly get tight? Or do you trust that everything will turn out alright? If you tend to worry, contemplating benevolence can shift you back to a place of trusting that everything _is_ okay and will be okay.

Take a moment to make a list of times when you experienced benevolence or kind gestures. Think back to a time when you received a generous gift, realized you were naturally talented at something, or experienced the gracious synchronicity of the universe itself. Benevolence also comes in the form of receiving help in a moment of need, being taken under a mentor's wing, or feeling loved when you need it most. Consider those experiences where it felt as if a benevolent force steered you in the right direction, dropped an idea into your creative flow, or pulled circumstances together in a series of remarkable coincidences. As you contemplate your experiences of benevolence, allow yourself to relax into that feeling. Notice how recalling benevolent experiences shifts your physical and mental state from worry into a receptive, grateful, and trusting feeling. If you find your mind wandering, continue to recall your experiences until you relax into positive feelings again.

Notice how your body, breath, and emotions feel when you contemplate benevolence. Did your shoulders release down? Did your breathing become easier and deeper? Are you smiling? Do you feel more receptive, trusting, at ease, and in flow? Create a mantra for yourself from your state. For example: I feel *trust* in the benevolent flow of my life.

You can adapt this tool by replacing benevolence with any positive state you'd like to cultivate: serenity, joy, empowerment, contentment, love, and so on.

NOTES

_____

_____

_____

_____

_____

_____

_____

Comforting C

Cache, Cadence, Calling, Calm, Can, Candor, Capable, Capstone,
Cardinal Virtues, Care, Carefree, Careful, Caress, Caring, Cash,
Castle, Celebrate, Centered, Certain, Certainty, Certitude, Chakra,
Challenge, Change, Chant, Charisma, Charm, Charitable, Charity,
Cheer, Cheerful, Chic, Child, Chime, Chlorophyll, Choice, Chosen,
Chrysalis, Civil, Civilization, Civilize, Civil Liberty, Clairvoyance,

Clarity, Classic, Clean, Clear, Clemency, Clement, Clever,
Close, Coach, Coalesce, Coherent, Collaborate, Color, Comedy,
Comfort, Comfortable, Comforting, Commend, Commitment,
Commune, Communication, Community, Companion,
Companionship, Compassion, Compassionate, Competent,
Complement, Compliment, Compose, Concentrate, Conception,
Conciliate, Confidence, Confident, Congenial, Congratulate,
Connect, Conscience, Conscientious, Conscious, Consciousness,
Considerate, Consistent, Console, Conspirito, Contemplate,
Content, Contribute, Convenient, Convivial, Cooperate, Cordial,
Cornucopia, Cosmic, Cosmology, Count, Courage, Courteous,
Courtesy, Cozy, Create, Creation, Creative, Credential, Cry,
Cultivate, Culture, Cure, Curious

ADD YOUR OWN GOLDEN C WORDS

_____

_____

_____

_____

_____

CACHE: A hiding place to safeguard valuables
CADENCE: A rhythmic flow, such as in music, dance, or poetry
CALLING: An inner longing for a specific occupation or profession
CALM: Composed, quiet, still, serene, peaceful

CAN: The ability to do something; the power, means, or right

CANDOR: Straightforward, sincere, truth

CAPABLE: The capacity to do something, competent

CAPSTONE: A crowning achievement, high point

CARDINAL VIRTUES: Justice, fortitude, temperance, prudence

CARE: To protect, attend to, or be concerned about something
or someone

CAREFREE: To be free of worry or concern

CAREFUL: Cautious, protective

CARESS: A gentle touch done with love, fondness, or affection

CARING: Having compassion and concern for others

CASH: Paper or coin representing payment in exchange for
services or goods

CASTLE: A palace; private refuge

CELEBRATE: To acknowledge an event with appropriate activity
or ceremony

CENTERED: Well-balanced, confident

CERTAIN: Dependable, positive, assured

CERTAINTY: Confidence, conviction

CERTITUDE: Certain

CHAKRA: A spiritual center in the body corresponding to
a nerve plexus

CHALLENGE: Requiring the use of one's resources, talents, and abilities

CHANGE: To transform an appearance, a feeling, or a condition
into something different

CHANT: A short simple melody sung in celebration

CHARISMA: A quality about someone that is magnetic

CHARM: A quality about something that fascinates and delights

CHARITABLE: Generous

CHARITY: Offering relief to someone in need

CHEER: Something that gives joy or happiness; encouragement

CHEERFUL: Being happy or pleasant

CHIC: Stylish, fashionable

CHILD: A young person

CHIME: A harmonious sound; agreement

CHLOROPHYLL: A green plant pigment found in plants that perform photosynthesis

CHOICE: Having options and alternatives

CHOSEN: Preferred above all others

CHRYSALIS: A hard case that protects a caterpillar while it turns into a butterfly; a stage of development or growth

CIVIL: Polite, courteous

CIVILIZATION: Human society marked by advanced development in the arts, sciences, with complexity in social, political, and cultural systems

CIVILIZE: Educate, enlighten, refine

CIVIL LIBERTY: Legal freedoms of speech, thought, and action guaranteed to an individual

CLAIRVOYANCE: Intuitive perception beyond the five senses; second sight

CLARITY: Lucidity, clearness

CLASSIC: An exceptional representative; significant worth; artist, author, or work that is outstanding in its class

CLEAN: Sanitary, fresh

CLEAR: Evident; free from flaw

CLEMENCY: Mild, lenient, and merciful in disposition and action

CLEMENT: Mild, merciful

CLEVER: Original, ingenious, mentally nimble

CLOSE: Connected by affection, friendship, and common interests

Coach: A teacher or tutor hired to educate, instruct, and encourage on a specific subject or skill

Coalesce: To come together, unite as one whole

Coherent: All parts of a system that make sense as a whole

Collaborate: To join together to accomplish something

Color: Reflected light of different hues, saturation, and brightness

Comedy: A humorous and light form of entertainment

Comfort: Ease, relief, and solace of pain; well-being

Comfortable: At ease, cozy, snug

Comforting: Soothing

Commend: To praise or recommend something that is worthy

Commitment: A pledge

Commune: To discuss intimately

Communication: An exchange of ideas

Community: A group of people living in proximity often with similar interests

Companion: A friend to spend time with

Companionship: Friendship

Compassion: Consideration, concern, kindness

Compassionate: Deeply feeling and sharing another person's suffering; showing mercy or support toward a person in need

Competent: Well-qualified for a specific purpose

Complement: Something added that enhances, improves, or perfects

Compliment: To express admiration, respect, or fondness

Compose: To make oneself peaceful, calm, serene; to create an aesthetic arrangement

Concentrate: To focus one's attention

Conception: The beginning or birth

Conciliate: To reconcile, soothe, or pacify

CONFIDENCE: Belief in oneself or another; conviction

CONFIDENT: Feeling assured of one's own abilities;
   feeling certain of the truth about someone or something

CONGENIAL: A personable, friendly, agreeable personality

CONGRATULATE: To express good wishes, praise, joy,
   or applause for someone's achievement

CONNECT: Joining together; bond, unite

CONSCIENCE: Inner guidance that recognizes right from wrong

CONSCIENTIOUS: Careful, thorough, scrupulous

CONSCIOUS: Aware of your own existence

CONSCIOUSNESS: The state of awareness of one's surroundings;
   perception of mental and emotional processes

CONSIDERATE: Thoughtful toward other people's feelings

CONSISTENT: Reliable

CONSOLE: To comfort during a challenging time

CONSPIRITO: With spirit, animated

CONTEMPLATE: To consider thoughtfully, intensively,
   and profoundly

CONTENT: Serenely happy with present circumstances; satisfied

CONTRIBUTE: To share in the giving for something

CONVENIENT: Suited to one's needs; easy and accessible

CONVIVIAL: A person who is friendly and joyful; an event that
   is lively, welcoming, and cheerful

COOPERATE: To work with others toward a common purpose or goal

CORDIAL: Friendly

CORNUCOPIA: Overflowing with abundance and prosperity,
   sometimes signified with a goat's horn (or similar object)
   filled with fruits, vegetables, and flowers

COSMIC: Vast, universal, harmonious; concerning the universe

COSMOLOGY: A branch of study that examines the origin and
   evolution of the universe

Count: To name with a series of numbers; to follow a beat in music; to believe in something; to have value

Courage: To face danger with strength, confidence, and valor from the heart

Courteous: Respectful toward others

Courtesy: Gracious behavior; good manners

Cozy: Snug, comfortable, warm, and relaxed

Create: To bring into existence

Creation: All that exists in the entire universe; a work of art

Creative: Possessing the ability to bring something into being

Credential: Earned qualification

Cry: To weep and shed tears

Cultivate: To nurture the growth of something

Culture: The beliefs, customs, attitudes, languages, arts, sciences, and other thoughts and institutions of a particular community; to grow something using a particular medium for nourishment

Cure: Recovery of health following a disease; a particular course of treatment or remedy that brings a disease into remission

Curious: Eager for knowledge and information

WRITE YOUR FAVORITE GOLDEN C WORDS HERE

_____

_____

_____

_____

_____

NOW USE YOUR FAVORITE GOLDEN C WORDS
TO CREATE YOUR OWN MANTRA OR AFFIRMATION

_____

_____

_____

_____

_____

Tool: Clean-Up Game

Breaking out of a mental habit takes practice, which may sound boring, like homework, but making it into a game can be fun. You can play this game any time you clean. You could be cleaning the house or your car, washing the dishes and kitchen sink after dinner, the birdbath (my weekly chore), or your gardening tools. Anything's game in the clean-up game.

The first step is to get your head in the game. Before you clean, take a deep breath in and hold that breath for a few seconds. Now gently release that breath. Repeat this two more times, then let your breath be natural. Choose a goal you'd like to accomplish, then create an intention to clear all the obstacles from your path as you clean so your goal becomes crystal clear, evident, and in the present moment.

While you clean, imagine each dust ball, piece of dirt, and food particle as a block or emotion you feel is in the way of reaching your goal. As you clean up, allow yourself to see and acknowledge every one of them. If you're cleaning the bathroom mirror, imagine that a smudge represents something someone said that made you feel you couldn't achieve your goal. Wipe it away until it's polished clean and your intention is clearly reflected back to you. With each act of cleaning, imagine clearing away physical symptoms, financial issues, old memories, or other concerns, allowing your confidence to rise and your path to be cleared. Watch worries, fears, pessimism, and roadblocks go up the vacuum, down the drain, onto your rags, into the trash or washing machine, hosed far away, or flushed down the toilet. Gone. Gone. Gone.

As concerns vanish, notice the clean surface and allow it to reflect your goal. In fact, imagine for a moment that you can see your future in the shiny, clean surface—like in a crystal ball. Imagine people cheering you on. Imagine events taking place as if your goal is real right now. Feel the joy of your accomplishment. See it in color. Listen to the sounds of success. Touch it with your hands. Know it to be true.

This tool brings joy and purpose to the mundane act of cleaning. As you clean all the dirty dishes, sweep away all the dust, and wash away all the tracked-in mud with your goal in mind, you're building physical and mental habits to support your goals.

NOTES

_____

_____

_____

_____

_____

_____

Delightful D

Dance, Daring, Darling, Daydream, Days of Grace, Dazzle, Dear, Death, Debonair, Decent, Decide, Decision, Decisive, Decorate, Dedicate, Dedicated, Deep, Deity, Deliberate, Delicacy, Delicious, Delight, Delightful, Delimit, Dependable, Deposit, Deserve, Desirable, Desire, Detached, Determine, Develop, Devotion, Dharma, Dialogue, Diamond, Dignity, Diligent, Direct, Direction,

Discipline, Discover, Discovery, Discreet, Discuss, Diversity, Divine, Do, Doctor, Dream, Dreamy, Drive, Duty, Dynamic

ADD YOUR OWN GOLDEN D WORDS

_____

_____

_____

_____

_____

Dance: Move in rhythm to music

Daring: Willing to take a risk; adventurous, courageous, bold

Darling: One who is loved, liked, or preferred; an affectionate term

Daydream: A reverie about a wish or hope

Days of Grace: Additional days given to pay a past due bill

Dazzle: To inspire wonder or amazement

Dear: A cherished or precious person; a term of affection

Death: Merging into light at the time of physical death

Debonair: A good disposition; courteous, affable

Decent: Kind

Decide: Make a choice; make up one's mind

Decision: The act of making a choice

Decisive: To settle without a doubt

Decorate: To embellish with beautiful objects

Dedicate: To set aside for a specific purpose; to commit fully

Dedicated: Devoted to a purpose, task, or person

DEEP: Profound

DEITY: Divinity

DELIBERATE: Done with careful thought and reflection; intentional

DELICACY: A choice, appealing food

DELICIOUS: Pleasing to the senses, especially smell and taste

DELIGHT: Joy, pleasure

DELIGHTFUL: Giving great joy

DELIMIT: Create boundaries

DEPENDABLE: Trustworthy

DEPOSIT: Trust with safekeeping, especially money in a bank

DESERVE: To be worthy, merit

DESIRABLE: Something that is preferred

DESIRE: To want

DETACHED: Disconnected

DETERMINE: To choose a direction

DEVELOP: To unfold or expand a potential

DEVOTION: Time and affection dedicated to a person or cause

DHARMA: Right conduct

DIALOGUE: A discussion among two or more people

DIAMOND: A crystalline gemstone

DIGNITY: Carrying oneself with self-respect

DILIGENT: Industrious

DIRECT: To give guidance toward a specific goal; the shortest way

DIRECTION: A particular course taken

DISCIPLINE: Controlling one's behavior in order to reach a certain goal

DISCOVER: To observe, find, and learn

DISCOVERY: A finding

DISCREET: Tactful

DISCUSS: To talk with someone or a group

DIVERSITY: Variety

DIVINE: Heavenly, delightful, of God

Do: To carry out an action

Doctor: A person with advanced training; a teacher

Dream: An aspiration or wish; a beautiful image

Dreamy: Serene

Drive: Determination to create or do something

Duty: A moral responsibility

Dynamic: Lively, energetic, vibrant

WRITE YOUR FAVORITE GOLDEN D WORDS HERE

_____

_____

_____

_____

_____

NOW USE YOUR FAVORITE GOLDEN D WORDS TO CREATE YOUR OWN MANTRA OR AFFIRMATION

_____

_____

_____

_____

_____

Tool: Opening Doors

What comes to mind when you think about doors? Does one door close while another door opens? Do you picture potential prizes behind Door #1, Door #2, or Door #3? Do you imagine the wooden door of a home, the glass door on a store, the quaint door of an inn, automatic doors on grocery stores, sliding doors to a backyard, fire doors in a hospital, the fortress doors on a castle, or the entrance to a cave? What about the door to your subconscious, the doorway to another realm, or the doors of opportunity? Have you ever considered doorways to your imagination, health, prosperity, love, peace, or friendship?

In a hypnosis-coaching session, I often bring my clients to the doorway of their subconscious or to doors that open to other areas of their lives to find out more about their inner resources. Each person's doors look different; the information inside is unique to their own situation and questions. Some people have ornate wooden doors with round brass pulls, other people have retracting doors that clang open and closed. Some are painted doors, yet others are simple entryways.

Once you go through that door, messages from your subconscious may come as images, words, sounds, smells, or feelings. You may see someone you know who symbolizes something important to you. Familiar objects or symbols may present themselves or something may come to you that you've never heard of before.

In this tool, you can open a door to anything you choose. For the purpose of this example, let's choose the doorway to your subconscious, where valuable information is stored for your support. Once inside your subconscious, you can ask for information related to any goal you're working on such as improved health, prosperity, completion of a project, or insight on a relationship. Choose a goal now. Keep a journal by your side so you can write down your insights, or talk through your experience on a recording device and listen to it afterward.

Close your eyes and relax. Take a few deep breaths in through your nose and out through your nose or mouth. Then allow your breathing to become deep, slow, and natural. Imagine you're taking a walk in your favorite place in nature: the beach, the woods, the desert, a winter wonderland, or the mountains. It's your favorite season and time of day. Be aware of your environment through all your senses as you relax and enjoy your walk. Take your time to listen to the sounds, feel the breeze, smell the fresh air, and notice the details of the landscape that you enjoy so much.

As you walk, you come to a door. As you approach the door, notice the details. Someone may be there to open the door for you, or it may open as you approach it. Go through the opening; look around. What do you notice? Is anyone there? Take your time to move through your surroundings. Tune in and observe.

When you feel like you've received all the information you need, thank your subconscious and go back to your walk. Gradually become aware of the sounds around you, your physical environment, and your body in contact with your chair. Take notes in your journal or listen to the recording of your experience. Reflect on how you'll incorporate what you've learned.

NOTES

_____

_____

_____

_____

_____

Effortless E

Eager, Earn, Earnest, Earth, Ease, Easily, Easy, Eat, Ebullient, Eccentric, Ecology, Ecosystem, Ecstasy, Ecstatic, Edible, Educate, Education, Educational, Effect, Effective, Effervescent, Efficacious, Efficient, Effort, Effortless, Effulgent, Effuse, Ego, Elaborate, Elate, Electric, Electricity, Elegant, Elevate, Elixir, Eloquent, Elucidate, Emancipate, Embody, Embrace, Emerge, Eminent, Emotion, Empathy, Empower, Emulate, Enable, Enamor, Enchant,

Encompass, Encourage, Endear, Endeavor, Endurance, Energetic, Energize, Energy, Engage, Engaging, Engross, Enjoy, Enlighten, Enliven, Enormous, Enough, Enrich, Ensoul, Enterprising, Enthrall, Enthusiasm, Entrance, Entrust, Epiphany, Equality, Equanimity, Equilibrium, Equitable, Equity, Esprit, Essence, Essential, Esteem, Eternal, Ethereal, Ethical, Eudemonics, Euphonious, Euphoria, Evolve, Exalt, Exceed, Excel, Excellent, Exceptional, Excited, Exemplar, Exemplary, Exercise, Exhilarate, Expand, Expect, Expectant, Experience, Experiment, Expertise, Exploration, Explore, Express, Exquisite, Extra, Extraordinary, Extrovert, Exuberant, Exultant

ADD YOUR OWN GOLDEN E WORDS

_____

_____

_____

_____

_____

EAGER: Enthusiastic, desirous, expectant

EARN: To receive something in return for providing a service or product

EARNEST: Determined; having purpose or strong intent

EARTH: Soil for planting; our planetary home

EASE: Comfort; freedom from challenge or pain

EASILY: Effortlessly

EASY: Able to accomplish something in a relaxed manner

EAT: To take in nourishment through the mouth

EBULLIENT: Brimming with excitement, enthusiasm

ECCENTRIC: Different than the norm

ECOLOGY: The science of understanding the relationship between living things and the environment

ECOSYSTEM: Interdependent organisms in the environment

ECSTASY: Intense rapture, elation, delight, exaltation

ECSTATIC: Feeling intense rapture, elation, delight, exaltation

EDIBLE: Safe to be eaten

EDUCATE: To teach; to provide with knowledge

EDUCATION: Formal or informal instruction to impart skills, knowledge, and understanding

EDUCATIONAL: Informative; enlightening

EFFECT: The power to influence

EFFECTIVE: Producing a desired outcome

EFFERVESCENT: High-spirited, energetic, vivacious

EFFICACIOUS: Able to produce the intended effect; effective

EFFICIENT: Effective without waste

EFFORT: Using physical and/or mental energy to accomplish something

EFFORTLESS: Accomplished with little to no effort

EFFULGENT: Shining brilliantly

EFFUSE: To radiate, to flow out

EGO: The personality, the conscious self

ELABORATE: To work out the details thoroughly with care

ELATE: In high spirits, overjoyed, delighted

ELECTRIC: Exciting emotionally

ELECTRICITY: A state of excitement; emotional charge

ELEGANT: Refined, graceful

ELEVATE: To raise up to a higher level

ELIXIR: A potion with curative, healing powers

ELOQUENT: Verbally expressive; articulate

ELUCIDATE: To make clear, clarify

EMANCIPATE: Free from bondage; liberate

EMBODY: To incarnate

EMBRACE: To hug with affection

EMERGE: To rise forth from obscurity

EMINENT: Outstanding in character or achievement

EMOTION: A strong feeling

EMPATHY: Understanding the thoughts and feelings of another

EMPOWER: To endow with power

EMULATE: To imitate someone to achieve or go beyond
their level of excellence

ENABLE: To make something possible

ENAMOR: To inspire with love

ENCHANT: To delight, captivate

ENCOMPASS: To include

ENCOURAGE: To support and inspire someone with confidence

ENDEAR: To make yourself liked or beloved

ENDEAVOR: A conscientious effort to achieve something

ENDURANCE: Perseverance in a time of challenge

ENERGETIC: Full of vigor; animated

ENERGIZE: Activate; fill with energy

ENERGY: Vitality; capable of action

ENGAGE: To participate, get involved

ENGAGING: Charming

ENGROSS: To be completely absorbed

ENJOY: To feel pleasure from an experience

ENLIGHTEN: To impart knowledge, truth, spiritual understanding

ENLIVEN: To animate, fill with spirit

ENORMOUS: Huge

ENOUGH: Sufficient for the purpose

ENRICH: Enhance; to make rich with good feeling, money, information, or meaning

ENSOUL: Endow with a soul

ENTERPRISING: Showing initiative, resourcefulness in an endeavor

ENTHRALL: To captivate one's attention

ENTHUSIASM: Intense interest and enjoyment

ENTRANCE: To put in a trance; to fascinate

ENTRUST: To put your trust in someone

EPIPHANY: A sudden flash of understanding

EQUALITY: Having equal rights

EQUANIMITY: Characteristic of even-mindedness, composure

EQUILIBRIUM: A system that is stable, balanced

EQUITABLE: Impartial, fair

EQUITY: Fairness

ESPRIT: Liveliness of spirit; vivacious

ESSENCE: The intrinsic nature of someone or something

ESSENTIAL: Fundamental

ESTEEM: To regard favorably

ETERNAL: Existing beyond time; having no beginning or end

ETHEREAL: Light, refined, exquisite

ETHICAL: In accordance with moral standards

EUDEMONICS: The art of living a happy life

EUPHONIOUS: A sound that is agreeable

EUPHORIA: Bliss; tremendous happiness or well-being

EVOLVE: To make progress in one's development

EXALT: To fill with joy and delight

EXCEED: To surpass

EXCEL: To do well at something

EXCELLENT: Of high quality

EXCEPTIONAL: Extraordinary

EXCITED: An increase of energy

EXEMPLAR: A model of high quality

EXEMPLARY: Ideal

EXERCISE: Physical or mental activity

EXHILARATE: Invigorate with life energy

EXPAND: To open up, develop, or unfold

EXPECT: Looking forward to

EXPECTANT: Waiting for the birth of a child

EXPERIENCE: Participation in life events

EXPERIMENT: To test an idea

EXPERTISE: Expert skill, specialized knowledge

EXPLORATION: Investigation of the unknown

EXPLORE: Discover; travel; search

EXPRESS: To communicate ideas with words, gestures, or movements

EXQUISITE: Extremely beautiful

EXTRA: Beyond what is expected

EXTRAORDINARY: Beyond the commonplace

EXTROVERT: An outgoing person

EXUBERANT: High-spirited; overjoyed

EXULTANT: Triumphant, victorious, thrilled

WRITE YOUR FAVORITE GOLDEN E WORDS HERE

_____

_____

_____

_____

_____

NOW USE YOUR FAVORITE GOLDEN E WORDS TO CREATE YOUR OWN MANTRA OR AFFIRMATION

_____

_____

_____

_____

_____

Tool: Equanimity in Balance

Many people come for hypnosis so they can experience equanimity during the ups and downs of their lives. Can you remember a time when you felt challenged, yet remained composed? Perhaps you stay calm under certain types of pressure or during emergencies, but being human, you likely experience some life situations that get under your skin to one degree or another—situations where remaining calm is a challenge. If you'd like to experience more equanimity, more emotional balance in those situations, here's a technique you can practice.

Close your eyes and drift back to a time when you felt completely balanced and calm. As an aid, I suggest recalling an experience of physical balance such as riding a bicycle or skateboard; surfing, roller skating, or ice skating; walking a balance beam; standing on a balance board; or a similar balancing activity that suits you. Creating this state of physical balance stimulates emotional calm, deepens the breath, and produces calm alertness. When you're in physical balance, you're also "in your own space" and less likely to lean into the volatility of someone else's stress.

Choose the experience of physical balance you relate to best and allow the feeling of balance from your muscle memory to permeate your breathing, your body, and your mind for about a minute. Some people need to stand up in order to lock onto this experience. If you need to stand, please do so. Your eyes can be open or closed. Take notice of your breath, what you feel in your body, and your growing state of equanimity. You may feel your body shifting internally, as it does when you find your balance, then coming into a state of equilibrium. You may even yawn and feel your shoulders relax down.

Once you've created a feeling of physical balance in your body, think of a situation or a person that takes you off-balance, for example, a pattern at work or in a relationship that feels stressful or frustrating. I've used this technique for myself in interactions with people who tend to complain or anger easily. I've also coached people to use this technique in work situations with stressed customers. Choose the situation you want to work with, then imagine or "project" the situation or person onto an imaginary movie screen in front of yourself. Imagine this screen as far away as needed for you to remain balanced.

Observe the situation or person on your imaginary screen while staying focused on remaining balanced. Witnessing the situation or person on this imaginary screen from a state of physical balance will automatically create some emotional distance and composure. From this state of equanimity in balance, observe any changes or movements that take place in the movie images.

If at any time you lose your sense of balance and need to reconnect to the feeling of equanimity, redirect your attention back to the experience you used to achieve physical balance. Once you're in balance again, return to observing your movie.

Practice for a few minutes every day until you can stay balanced and a new perspective emerges while in the imagined presence of your challenging situation or person. This happens quickly for most people. Plan to remain balanced in equanimity when these situations come up in your life so you're prepared. When you implement this tool in a real-life situation, find your balance, take a small step back if necessary to feel comfortable, and stay in your space of balance. Notice how much more composed you feel in the situation by using physical balance to maintain equanimity. Notice, too, how much more conscious control you have over your response.

You can repeat this activity for any person or situation that takes you off balance. Practice toward a sense of mastery in each situation where you'd like to experience equanimity in balance.

NOTES

_____

_____

_____

_____

_____

_____

Fortuitous F

Fabulous, Facile, Facilitate, Fair, Faith, Faithful, Fame, Family,
Fantastic, Fascinate, Fashion, Father, Favor, Favorable, Fear, Fearless,
Feasible, Feisty, Felicity, Fertile, Festive, Fidelity, Finance, Fine,
Finesse, Finish, Fire, First-class, Fit, Flexible, Flexibility, Flight,
Float, Flora, Floral, Flourish, Flow, Flower, Fluid, Focus, Fond,
Food, Foresee, Foreshadow, Foresight, Forest, Forget, Forgive, Form,
Formidable, Forthright, Fortify, Fortitude, Fortuitous, Forward,

Foster, Four-leaf Clover, Fragrant, Free, Freedom, Fresh, Friend,
Friendly, Friendship, Frolic, Frugal, Fruition, Fulfill, Full, Fun,
Fundamental, Funeral, Furnish, Future

ADD YOUR OWN GOLDEN F WORDS

_____

_____

_____

_____

_____

FABULOUS: Legendary, astonishing

FACILE: Arrived at easily; easy

FACILITATE: To ease the way; to free from obstacles

FAIR: Beautiful; impartial, just

FAITH: Confidence in the truth, without need for material evidence

FAITHFUL: Reliable; worthy of trust; believable

FAME: The condition of being well-known

FAMILY: Kin, ancestral lineage; social group

FANTASTIC: Wondrous, remarkable

FASCINATE: To strongly hold one's interest; captivate

FASHION: To mold or create in a specific form

FATHER: A male parent

FAVOR: An act of kindness

FAVORABLE: Helpful, advantageous, auspicious

FEAR: Anxiety or apprehension

Fearless: Courageous

Feasible: Able to be accomplished

Feisty: Spunky, spirited

Felicity: Abundant happiness; bliss

Fertile: Productive, prolific, bountiful

Festive: Merry

Fidelity: Faithful to one's duties, loyal

Finance: Money management

Fine: Of high quality; precise; satisfactory

Finesse: Subtlety, tact, discretion

Finish: Complete, attain

Fire: Enthusiasm, brilliance, warmth

First-class: Excellent, first-rate

Fit: Physically healthy; well-adapted

Flexible: Adaptable; pliable, bendable

Flexibility: The ability to adapt

Flight: A journey that transcends limitations

Float: Hover, soar; to remain suspended on a surface or in the air without support

Flora: Plants, vegetation

Floral: Reminiscent of flowers

Flourish: To thrive, prosper; to grow luxuriously, abundantly

Flow: To move with fluidity and ease

Flower: Bloom, blossom; develop fully

Fluid: Smooth, effortless

Focus: A point of concentration

Fond: Affectionate, loving, caring

Food: Plant or animal able to be ingested for nourishment

Foresee: To envision beforehand

Foreshadow: To know beforehand due to a suggestion or clue

FORESIGHT: Looking forward thoughtfully

FOREST: Trees in great quantity over a large expanse of land

FORGET: To remove from memory

FORGIVE: To pardon; let go of anger or resentment

FORM: To take shape; manifestation

FORMIDABLE: Awe-inspiring; daunting

FORTHRIGHT: Straightforward, direct, plainspoken

FORTIFY: To reinforce with strength

FORTITUDE: Strength of mind in a challenging time

FORTUITOUS: Happens by chance, without plan

FORWARD: Bold, progressive; eager

FOSTER: To nurture or promote someone's development

FOUR-LEAF CLOVER: A sign of good luck

FRAGRANT: A sweet scent as from a flower

FREE: Unrestricted

FREEDOM: Liberty

FRESH: Novel; recently harvested; invigorating

FRIEND: Someone who is liked, trusted,
    and regarded affectionately

FRIENDLY: Welcoming

FRIENDSHIP: A mutual alliance

FROLIC: High-spirited, lighthearted play

FRUGAL: Thrifty

FRUITION: Achievement of a desired outcome

FULFILL: To realize a goal; to bring a desire into reality

FULL: Complete; containing as much as normally possible

FUN: Enjoyment, pleasure, amusement

FUNDAMENTAL: Providing a base for; foundational

FUNERAL: A ceremony held to bury a loved one

FURNISH: To provide with what's needed

FUTURE: That which is to come

WRITE YOUR FAVORITE GOLDEN **F** WORDS HERE

_____

_____

_____

_____

_____

NOW USE YOUR FAVORITE GOLDEN **F** WORDS
TO CREATE YOUR OWN MANTRA OR AFFIRMATION

_____

_____

_____

_____

_____

Tool: The Funeral Service

Everyone experiences loss–of loved ones and cherished pets, life dreams, relationships, jobs, and health. We have funeral services to celebrate the contributions and qualities of our loved ones, mourn the loss we feel from their absence, and integrate the event into our consciousness. But what about other losses? How have you mourned those? In the busy rush of daily life, grieving important losses often gets pushed aside. But the grief stays with us, gnawing at us in various ways, waiting to be processed.

First, find a comfortable, private place to sit, then close your eyes. Privacy is important because you'll speak aloud during this process. Take a few slow, deep breaths in through your nose and out through your nose or mouth. Allow your breath to become natural, deep, and slow. Choose something you need to mourn. Or just allow it to rise to the surface, gently.

Start with one loss, and see where it takes you. This could be the loss of a life dream, an aspect of your health, a financial goal, a relationship, a job, or anything important that comes to mind. If you haven't fully mourned the loss of a person, let that come up for you.

Imagine yourself in a cemetery. This may be a cemetery you know or one your imagination invents. The cemetery is peaceful, with tombstones that represent a variety of losses. You can read the print on these tombstones and when you do, you realize you're not alone. So many people have shared similar losses in their lives.

Soon you come upon a grave that's been dug to bury your loss. There's a comfortable chair for you to sit down while you give your eulogy. Place your loss into the grave and remember. Remember all the gifts and say them aloud. Remember all the challenges and say them aloud. As you proceed through your spontaneous speech, allow all your thoughts and insights to flow.

Now contemplate what followed that loss. How have you moved on? What strengths did you develop? What personality attributes grew from the experience? If you're mourning the loss of a person, what qualities have you cultivated that you admired in that person? What goals did you set? What accomplishments did you attain? What gifts, if any, came from this loss?

Now ask the loss if there's anything else it would like to share with you before you bury it. Be open to receiving insights from your loss in any form: images, sounds, symbols, additional memories, feelings, concepts, inspirations, and so on.

After receiving your insights, toss a shovelful of earth into the grave.
Continue shoveling until your loss is buried. Perhaps others come along
to help you with the burial process. Now place a headstone on the grave
and imagine the words you'd like to place there. When the ceremony is
complete, return your awareness to your breath and gradually open your
eyes. Take notes on your insights and visit the cemetery as often as you
wish to honor your loss and bury other ones.

NOTES

_____

_____

_____

_____

_____

_____

Gorgeous G

Gaiety, Gaily, Gain, Gainful, Gallant, Garden, Gateway, Gather, Gay, Gelt, Gem, Generate, Generous, Generosity, Genial, Genius, Gentleman, Genuine, Gentle, Gestalt, Gift, Giggle, Give, Give-and-take, Giving, Glad, Glee, Glorious, Glory, Glow, God, Goddess, Godhood, Godly, Gold, Golden, Good, Good-hearted, Good-humored, Good-natured, Goodness, Good-tempered, Goody,

Gorgeous, Grace, Gracious, Grand, Grant, Grateful, Gratitude, Gravity, Gravy Train, Great, Greet, Grin, Ground, Grounded, Grow, Growth, Guardian, Guidance, Guide, Guru

ADD YOUR OWN GOLDEN G WORDS

_____

_____

_____

_____

_____

GAIETY: Cheerfulness, merriment

GAILY: Done in a joyful manner

GAIN: Achieved, earned, or acquired

GAINFUL: Profitable

GALLANT: Courageous, valiant, brave

GARDEN: Land used to cultivate flowers, trees, shrubs, fruits and vegetables, often for pleasure

GATEWAY: An entryway

GATHER: To come together as in people, ideas, flowers, materials

GAY: Exuberant, mirthful, carefree

GELT: Yiddish slang for money

GEM: A semi-precious or precious stone that may be cut and polished; a person or thing of value

GENERATE: To produce; to originate

GENEROUS: Willing to share; abundant, plentiful

GENEROSITY: Unselfish giving

GENIAL: Kindly disposition; cordial, gracious

GENIUS: Exceptional in intelligence, talent, creativity

GENTLEMAN: A polite, well-mannered man

GENUINE: Authentic

GENTLE: Considerate, mild, soft, tender, placid

GESTALT: A whole that is more than the sum of its parts

GIFT: Something that is given voluntarily, a present; a talent

GIGGLE: Chuckle

GIVE: To offer, bestow, or present something to someone

GIVE-AND-TAKE: An exchange of ideas resulting in compromise and cooperation

GIVING: Charitable

GLAD: Experiencing joy, cheerful

GLEE: Merriment, joy, happiness, laughter

GLORIOUS: Magnificent, delightful, splendid

GLORY: Splendor

GLOW: Shine radiantly

GOD: The spirit that pervades the universe

GODDESS: A woman seen as having great beauty that arises from her connection to Spirit

GODHOOD: Sensing one's own connection to God or Spirit

GODLY: Having respect for God

GOLD: Riches; a valuable metal; perceived as valuable

GOLDEN: Radiant; favorable; marked by prosperity, peace, and good fortune

GOOD: Having positive qualities; desirable; worthy; upright

GOOD-HEARTED: Generous and kind

GOOD-HUMORED: Cheerful, friendly

GOOD-NATURED: Having a cheerful and friendly disposition

Goodness: Worthiness, virtuousness

Good-tempered: Having an easygoing disposition

Goody: A delectable treat

Gorgeous: Magnificent, stunning, strikingly attractive

Grace: Elegance in form or movement; protection by a benevolent force

Gracious: Kind, compassionate, courteous, and well-mannered

Grand: Large in scope; splendid; impressive

Grant: To consent or confer

Grateful: Thankful, appreciative

Gratitude: Expressing thanks for something received such as a gift or kindness

Gravity: The force exerted that keeps our feet on the ground

Gravy Train: A job that requires less effort for substantial profit

Great: Significant, meaningful

Greet: To welcome with respect

Grin: A wide smile

Ground: To make gains in an area of endeavor; to stick with your principles or decision

Grounded: Practical, sensible, balanced

Grow: To flourish, thrive, and develop

Growth: The process of developing

Guardian: One who protects

Guidance: Advice, counsel

Guide: Someone with greater experience who shows the way or advises

Guru: A spiritual guide

WRITE YOUR FAVORITE GOLDEN **G** WORDS HERE

NOW USE YOUR FAVORITE GOLDEN **G** WORDS TO CREATE YOUR OWN MANTRA OR AFFIRMATION

Tool: Breathe in a Flower Garden

Between driving in cars, working in buildings, and exercising in health clubs, most people don't get much fresh air. Add to that the poor air quality in most buildings and busy streets. You may not even connect symptoms such as brain fog, fatigue, headaches, or nausea to living and working without fresh air, especially once you become used to doing so. Another consequence of keeping your life closed up is shallow breathing.

This exercise will teach you how to breathe more deeply using your creative imagination.

Part 1

Find a place to sit down and relax. You can also do this lying down. Close your eyes and imagine you're in the most beautiful garden full of fragrant flowers and herbs as far as the eye can see. They can be real ones such as roses, jasmine, gardenias, blossoming orange trees, or any other fragrant flowers you like. The herbs may be familiar, like basil, rosemary, sage, or ones you'd find deeper in the woods. Your garden can also have imaginary flowers whose blossoms are as large as dinner plates, the color of rainbows, or made of shimmering colors. Your imaginary herbs can have fragrant leaves and flowers of any shape and color.

As you stroll through your garden, exotic and familiar fragrances drift past, and you feel more and more relaxed. Then you find yourself drawn to a particular flower or herb. You lean over to sniff, and experience the most delicious scent. Allow the fragrance to wash over you inside and out like a purifying bath. Then exhale completely through your nose or mouth. Continue to walk through the garden and deeply inhale the delicious fragrances of your favorite blossoms and herbs. Let each fragrance wash over and through you, clearing concerns from your body and mind. Repeat slowly three to eight times, or until you feel refreshed and relaxed.

Part 2

If you're able to walk and the weather is suitable, get yourself to the nearest botanical garden. If there's no botanical garden nearby, you can choose a park or a forest preserve. The idea is to find a place to walk where there are fresh air and plants that stimulate you to breathe. Make a commitment to walk or be outside for at least an hour, weather permitting.

If there's a garden or greenhouse, practice your flower breathing as you walk around and look at the plants and herbs. As you continue walking, notice your head clearing, your energy expanding, and your mind generating solutions to stressful problems. Being out of doors not only provides life-giving oxygen that clears and heals the body, but also reminds you of the larger world and universe. This distracts the mind from problems long enough to reduce their importance, allows the subconscious space to generate solutions, and quiets the mind so you can pay attention to your intuition.

When you walk and practice breathing with flowers or other plants, you build the habit of breathing deeply. As your habit grows, you'll begin to breathe more deeply without imagining flowers, though it's a bonus to stop and smell the roses. If possible, walk outdoors everyday. If daily walking isn't practical, then aim for three times a week. Even once a week is helpful to clear your head, encourage you to breathe deeply, and bring life-giving oxygen to your body.

NOTES

_____

_____

_____

_____

_____

Hello H

Ha, Habitable, Haiku, Hallelujah, Hallmark, Halo, Hand, Handsome, Happy, Happy-go-lucky, Harmonious, Harmony, Harvest, Have, Heal, Health, Healthy, Heart, Hearten, Heartfelt, Heartily, Heart-to-heart, Heartwarming, Hearty, Heaven, Heedful, Hello, Help, Helpful, Hero, Heroine, Hilarious, Holy, Home, Honest, Honor, Honorable, Hope, Hospitable, House,

Huge, Human, Humane, Humanity, Humanitarian, Humble, Humility, Humor, Humorous, Hygienic, Hypnogogic, Hypnosis, Hypnotherapy

ADD YOUR OWN GOLDEN H WORDS

_____

_____

_____

_____

_____

HA: An exclamation meant to express joy, surprise, or triumph

HABITABLE: A place that is suitable for living in; livable, comfortable

HAIKU: A 17-syllable Japanese poem that expresses the poet's feelings about nature

HALLELUJAH: An expression of great joy or praise

HALLMARK: A symbol of excellence or quality

HALO: A ring of light around the head of a saint or sacred figure

HAND: Applause; assistance, help

HANDSOME: Pleasing in appearance, attractive; generous

HAPPY: Showing pleasure, joy, or contentment

HAPPY-GO-LUCKY: Carefree, easygoing

HARMONIOUS: Melodic; well-balanced

HARMONY: When the parts of a whole create a pleasing or agreeable combination

HARVEST: Gathering a crop

HAVE: To win a victory

HEAL: To restore, to make whole; to reconcile or set right

HEALTH: The normal functioning of an organism; vigor, well-being

HEALTHY: Enjoying wellness in body, mind, and spirit; conducive to well-being

HEART: The seat of love and spirit within a person; someone prized as lovable

HEARTEN: Encourage, fill with strength

HEARTFELT: Felt deeply

HEARTILY: Warmly, completely

HEART-TO-HEART: Personal

HEARTWARMING: Uplifting, encouraging

HEARTY: Expressed with exuberance and sincerity

HEAVEN: A state of ecstasy; a place where angels and the divine reside; our Earth

HEEDFUL: Thoughtful, careful

HELLO: A friendly greeting

HELP: To lend a hand, assist

HELPFUL: Beneficial

HERO/HEROINE: Someone celebrated for bravery and courage

HILARIOUS: Hysterically funny

HOLY: Associated with the sacred, divine

HOME: A valued shelter of love and happiness

HONEST: Trustworthy, sincere, honorable

HONOR: Integrity, distinction

HONORABLE: Deserving of respect and honor

Hope: To wish for something with expectation and confidence in its fulfillment

Hospitable: To welcome guests with kindness and warmth

House: A dwelling

Huge: Tremendous

Human: A person

Humane: Having decent human qualities such as kindness, mercy, and compassion

Humanity: Human beings

Humanitarian: Concerned with alleviating the suffering of humanity

Humble: Showing modesty as opposed to pride

Humility: Modesty

Humor: Something intended to bring about laughter

Humorous: Inciting laughter; comical

Hygienic: Sanitary; cleanliness for the promotion of health

Hypnogogic: The state of drowsiness just before sleep

Hypnosis: An induced trance state where a person is open to suggestion by the hypnotist

Hypnotherapy: Therapy employing hypnosis

WRITE YOUR FAVORITE GOLDEN H WORDS HERE

_____

_____

_____

_____

_____

NOW USE YOUR FAVORITE GOLDEN H WORDS TO CREATE YOUR OWN MANTRA OR AFFIRMATION

_____

_____

_____

_____

_____

Tool: Enter Your Heart-Sanctuary

What is the connection for you between your heart and love? For me it is the flutter of my heart when I feel love, making hearts to give away on Valentine's Day as a child, and seeing initials carved on trees inside a heart shape when I was a teenager. Your heart chakra, which is located in the center of your chest just to the right of your physical heart, is the seat of love. When you experience your heart chakra opening, you feel love for no reason. No one has to do anything, say anything, or give you anything. Love just exists there as a pure, expansive, connecting force that flows as easily as a crystal-clear stream of water.

Place your hand on your belly, close your eyes, and take a deep breath in through your nose. Hold that breath deep inside for a few seconds, then gently exhale through your mouth or nose. Repeat, letting go of any anxiety or stress on each exhale. On your third breath, breathe in a golden light and allow that light to fill your body from your head to your toes and down to your fingertips. When your breath touches your fingertips, allow your shoulders to relax down. Breathe out golden light.

Feel your breath settle in your belly and become natural, breathing in golden light, breathing out golden light. Place your other hand on your heart chakra and become aware of how your breath touches that area as you breathe. Observe your breath massaging your heart chakra as you relax into your heart-space.

Now focus on the golden flame in the center of your heart. At first the flame might be small, like a glowing candle flame, but you can allow it to grow until it fills your entire chest with its warm light. Then allow the glow of the golden flame to expand until it envelops your entire being like a golden egg. As the flame continues to grow, allow it to become as large as a room you can walk around. This is your heart-sanctuary.

Take some time time to look around your heart-sanctuary. What do you observe? What is it made of? Is it constructed of crystals, precious stones, or carved wood? Is there a night sky with glittering stars or large puffy clouds in a blue sky? Is it like an old castle or an emerald forest with blue pools high on a mountaintop? Is there a path leading deeper into your sanctuary? Allow your heart-sanctuary to appear to you in the form that is unique for you.

Take your time and explore your heart-sanctuary. What is waiting for you there? Are there friendly guides who have a message for you? Is there a gift waiting for you to receive and use on your life-journey? Is your heart's love overflowing? Or is there something in the way of your flow that needs to be acknowledged and processed? Are you following your heart in your daily life or have you veered off your heart-path? Is there anything nagging at you that needs to be done to get back on your path? Take your time in your heart-sanctuary and do what's needed: clean house, listen and contemplate, receive, and rest.

Everything is okay in your heart-sanctuary. Everything is just as it should be. Sit quietly inside your golden flame, enjoying contentment for no reason whatsoever except that it's the nature of your heart. When you're ready to come back into physical awareness, you can bring the golden flame of your heart-sanctuary back into the center of your heart or leave it around yourself like a golden egg. Visit your heart to maintain it in the same way that you maintain your home.

NOTES

Inspirational I

Idea, Ideal, Idealist, Ideomotor, Idyllic, Illuminate, Imagination,
Immense, Immune, Imperfect, Impervious, Important, Impress,
Impressive, Improve, Incisive, Include, Income, Incomparable,
Incredible, Independent, Individuality, Indivisible, Ineffable,
Infinite, Infinity, Influence, Information, Ingenious, Inhabit,
Inherit, Inimitable, Initiate, Innate, Inner, Innocent, Innovate,

Inquire, Inscribe, Insight, Inspirational, Inspire, Inspirit, Instinct, Instruct, Instrument, Insure, Intact, Integrate, Integrity, Intellect, Intelligent, Intelligible, Intend, Intense, Intent, Intention, Interest, Interior, Internal, Intimate, Intrepid, Introspect, Intuition, Invaluable, Invent, Inventive, Invest, Invigorate, Invincible, Inviolable, Inviolate, Invite, Invocation, Invoke, Involved, Invulnerable, Inwardly, Irradiant

ADD YOUR OWN GOLDEN I WORDS

_____

_____

_____

_____

_____

IDEA: A thought or concept in the mind that exists in actuality
    or in potential
IDEAL: An exemplar; a standard of perfection that may
    or may not be attainable; a goal
IDEALIST: Visionary
IDEOMOTOR: A muscular activity in response to an ideation
    or mental image
IDYLLIC: Peaceful or heavenly
ILLUMINATE: To enlighten; to shine a light
IMAGINATION: The ability to form a creative mental concept
    or vision that is not currently present

IMMENSE: Boundless, huge

IMMUNE: Unaffected

IMPERFECT: Falling short of perfection

IMPERVIOUS: Not capable of being affected

IMPORTANT: Of great value; significant

IMPRESS: To create a deep influence

IMPRESSIVE: Awesome, remarkable

IMPROVE: To get better

INCISIVE: Keen perception, insightful

INCLUDE: To be a part of

INCOME: Money received in return for providing goods
     or services

INCOMPARABLE: Beyond comparison

INCREDIBLE: Astonishing

INDEPENDENT: Autonomous, self-reliant

INDIVIDUALITY: The uniqueness of a specific individual

INDIVISIBLE: Cannot be divided

INEFFABLE: Indescribable; beyond words

INFINITE, INFINITY: No limits in space or time

INFLUENCE: The power to affect a person or course of events

INFORMATION: Knowledge gathered from study, instruction,
     or experience

INGENIOUS: Having brilliance, an inventive mind

INHABIT: To occupy or dwell in

INHERIT: To receive a legacy, often material,
     from an ancestor

INIMITABLE: Unable to be imitated; unique

INITIATE: To be introduced to a skill or interest;
     to guide, instruct

INNATE: Essential

INNER: Occurring internally, privately

INNOCENT: Relatively pure; blameless

INNOVATE: To create or invent

INQUIRE: To examine closely in order to discover the truth

INSCRIBE: To write, print; dedicate as in a book or photo

INSIGHT: Understanding of the true nature of a person,
    thing, or situation

INSPIRATIONAL: Providing spiritual or creative guidance

INSPIRE: To motivate into action

INSPIRIT: To impart courage

INSTINCT: A deep-seated, inborn skill or behavior

INSTRUCT: To convey knowledge or information; educate

INSTRUMENT: A tool for measuring or making music

INSURE: To assure or make safe

INTACT: Whole

INTEGRATE: To unify, make whole

INTEGRITY: A code of behavior based on principles of honesty,
    honor, and reliability

INTELLECT: The capacity to reason; a mode of perception
    distinguished from feeling

INTELLIGENT: Having the ability to acquire knowledge
    and apply it

INTELLIGIBLE: Capable of being understood by the intellect

INTEND: To plan or design for a specific purpose

INTENSE: Deeply felt

INTENT: Application of attention to a specific purpose

INTENTION: A purpose that guides one's actions

INTEREST: Feeling curious or fascinated by something

INTERIOR: Relating to the inside, including one's spiritual being
    or center

INTERNAL: Located within; intrinsic

INTIMATE: Deeply familiar, essential

Intrepid: Fearless, bold

Introspect: Turn inward to examine one's thoughts and feelings

Intuition: Knowing something without the use of rational, cognitive processes

Invaluable: Of great value

Invent: To originate

Inventive: Creative, skillful at inventing

Invest: To commit time, money, or effort in order to gain a benefit later

Invigorate: To fill with vitality, strength, or vigor

Invincible: Unconquerable

Inviolable: Safe from profanity; sacred; intact

Inviolate: Intact; untouchable

Invite: A request for one's presence

Invocation: Calling upon a higher power for support, assistance

Invoke: Summon

Involved: Intricate

Invulnerable: Safe from attack; secure

Inwardly: Privately

Irradiant: Sending out light, shining

WRITE YOUR FAVORITE GOLDEN I WORDS HERE

_____

_____

_____

_____

_____

NOW USE YOUR FAVORITE GOLDEN I WORDS TO CREATE YOUR OWN MANTRA OR AFFIRMATION

_____

_____

_____

_____

_____

Tool: Invocation Prayer

Have you ever called upon a higher power to aid you in achieving something? Maybe you wanted to stop drinking alcohol or soft drinks, or give up sugar and junk food. Or maybe you lost a job, suffered from a dire illness, needed money for school, experienced bullying, or faced homelessness. Everyone has faced their own challenges and finds their own way to tap into their inner strength. For some people, it's through prayer.

Everyone who prays also finds his or her own approach to prayer. Some people believe that general prayers, like asking to receive blessings for their highest good, will give the best results. Other people believe that praying for something specific is more helpful. The type of prayer you'd like to voice is up to you.

1. **CHOOSE A TOPIC**: Contemplate what you most want to invoke guidance for in your life: health, love, confidence, inner strength, income, friendship, family, peace, and so on.

2. **CHOOSE GOLDEN WORDS**: Look through the words in this book until you find the ones that light you up.

WRITE THOSE WORDS HERE

_____

_____

_____

_____

_____

3. CREATE YOUR INVOCATION: Now create a prayer for yourself with those words. Speak from your heart as you play with the words aloud to craft your prayer. You'll feel strong emotion when you've found it.

4. OFFER PRAYER TO OTHERS: When you're finished, or if you're blessed with a life of complete contentment, consider invoking a higher power for the well-being of your community, country, or the planet using this process.

YOUR INVOCATION

_____

_____

_____

_____

_____

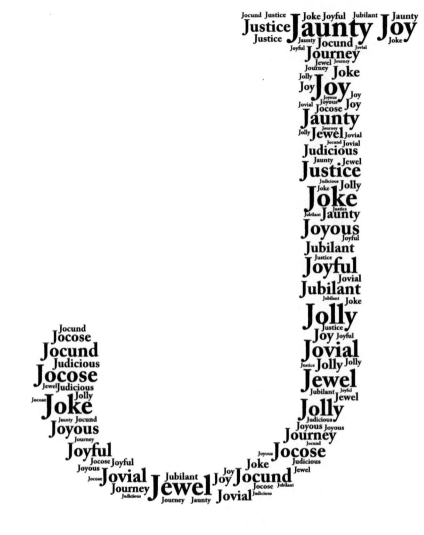

Joyful J

Jaunty, Jewel, Jocose, Jocund, Joke, Jolly, Journal, Journey, Jovial, Joy, Joyful, Joyous, Jubilant, Judicious, Just, Justice, Juvenescent

ADD YOUR OWN GOLDEN J WORDS

_____

_____

_____

_____

_____

JAUNTY: Carefree, self-confident

JEWEL: A gem, precious stone

JOCOSE: Humorous; known for joking

JOCUND: Having a lively, cheerful disposition

JOKE: A funny, amusing story

JOLLY: Fun-loving; festive

JOURNAL: A newspaper or magazine; a record
   of personal experiences and ideas

JOURNEY: Travel in the inner realms
   or the material world

JOVIAL: Cheerful, good-humored, convivial

JOY: A feeling of delight, happiness, or great pleasure

JOYFUL, JOYOUS: Full of joy and happiness

JUBILANT: Overjoyed; expressing triumphant joy

JUDICIOUS: Wise, cautious; sound judgment

JUST: Fair, moral, ethical
JUSTICE: Fair treatment
JUVENESCENT: Youthful

WRITE YOUR FAVORITE GOLDEN J WORDS HERE

_____

_____

_____

_____

_____

NOW USE YOUR FAVORITE GOLDEN J WORDS
TO CREATE YOUR OWN MANTRA OR AFFIRMATION

_____

_____

_____

_____

_____

Tool: Anchoring Joy

When life throws challenges your way, or when your busy schedule takes over, worry can be a killjoy. During times like these, joy waits on the sidelines for you to take a breather and fulfill your most basic need. Experiencing joy comes from more than just doing things you like or being with people you love; but also from getting the proper physical and emotional nourishment you need to feel your natural joy.

On a scale of 0 to 100, how much joy do you feel in your life? Take a moment to rate each area of your life in your journal or in the Joy Chart provided below under "Before Anchoring Joy." Which areas of life have you spent time cultivating? Which ones need attention?

Joy Chart

BEFORE ANCHORING JOY		AFTER ANCHORING JOY	
Relationships	_____	Relationships	_____
Career	_____	Career	_____
Fun	_____	Fun	_____
Home	_____	Home	_____
Finances	_____	Finances	_____
Spirituality	_____	Spirituality	_____
Creativity	_____	Creativity	_____
Health	_____	Health	_____

Choose an area of your life to contemplate where you've given joy a rating of at least 80 to 100. Drift into the experience of joy as you meditate on this part of your life. Allow the full physical and emotional experience of this joy. See, feel, taste, smell, and hear everything about your joy. When you feel at the peak of your joy, let go of the joyful experience you're contemplating and simply swim in the joy.

Notice how you experience joy in your body. Perhaps you feel tingly in your fingertips or toes, lighthearted, or notice your shoulders release down. Your breathing may be deep and relaxed. Your lips may turn up in a smile. When you feel at the peak of joy, notice where joy settles for you. In your belly? Your heart? Your smile? Place your hand on that place and create a phrase for yourself to anchor your joy. For example: I feel joy in my belly. I feel tingly joy in my toes. I feel automatic joy in my smile. I feel expansive joy in my heart.

After anchoring your joy, begin to contemplate an area of your life where you're not feeling the joy. Some uncomfortable feelings may arise, but stay with your joy and offer it to that part of your life. Literally bathe or wrap that part of your life in your joyousness. Observe the changes that take place as your worries and concerns are bathed in joy. Spread your joy, in turn, to each part of your life that needs more joy. Go back to the joyful areas of your life when you need refueling. Enjoy your joy. Take notes on any insights you have for making positive changes.

At the end of this exercise, go back to your joy rating and rate yourself again. How has your experience of joy shifted? As you gain insights and take action to make positive changes in areas of life where you want more joy, monitor your increases using the Joy Chart.

NOTES

_____

_____

_____

Kind K

Keen, Key, Kind, Kindly, Kindhearted,
Kinesthesia, Kiss, Know, Knowledge

ADD YOUR OWN GOLDEN K WORDS

_____

_____

_____

_____

_____

KEEN: Sharp intellect, fine perception; highly sensitive

KEY: Crucial information; answers to a test

KIND: Friendly, warmhearted, helpful; showing understanding
or sympathy to others

KINDLY: In a gentle manner

KINDHEARTED: Generosity coming from the heart

KINESTHESIA: The sensation of one's body and its position in space

KISS: To touch with the lips as a sign of affection

KNOW: To understand something with certainty

KNOWLEDGE: Information gained through education
or personal experience

WRITE YOUR FAVORITE GOLDEN K WORDS HERE

_____

_____

_____

_____

_____

NOW USE YOUR FAVORITE GOLDEN K WORDS
TO CREATE YOUR OWN MANTRA OR AFFIRMATION

_____

_____

_____

_____

Tool: Kinesthesia—Your Body Knows

How do you know things? Do you have an intuitive instinct? Do you require mountains of evidence and double-blind placebo-based studies to know? Do you believe only in what you can know with your five senses? Do you know based on what you've learned from experience? Do you learn from other people's experiences?

There are many ways to know something; a double-blind placebo-based study is one. Our five senses are important guides for getting information from our environment, and this knowledge can keep us safe. For example, we can keep ourselves healthy by testing whether food tastes right and air smells right, whether our environment looks and sounds right, and how warm or cold weather feels to our bodies. But in many life situations, even after obtaining a lot of information, many people will say, "It still didn't feel right so I went with my *gut*." In their own way, our bodies give us important signals to inform us of whether we're safe or in harm's way.

I had the opportunity to consult with a therapist about a woman whose baby was presenting in breech position a couple of days before the expected delivery date. In hypnosis, the expectant mother could sense the baby's reluctance to come into the world. She realized that reluctance came from marital tension in her home. She made a decision to take responsibility to resolve that tension and communicated to the baby that she was loved and welcomed into their home. The baby turned and the birth proceeded normally.

This unborn baby knew what was happening around her. She could feel and sense her environment and the people in it. As we grow up, we learn all different ways of knowing, and our visceral knowledge can get lost in the shuffle. Consider how your body feels in relation to the people and activities in your life. Do you feel like you're in breech position in some situations, but soldier on because you've learned to push past your body's wisdom?

Find a comfortable place to sit and relax. Take a deep breath in through your nose and hold it for a few seconds. Release your breath through your nose or mouth along with any stress you might feel. Think about a situation where you feel in a metaphorical breech position. Where in your body do you feel it? Does your heart flutter with anxiety? Do you get a sick feeling in the pit of your stomach? Does your throat close up?

Mentally, take a step back from the situation until you're far enough away to feel comfortable. To get mental distance, you can imagine the challenging situation getting smaller and smaller. You can also place an object that represents the situation on a table in front of you to remove it from your mental space. If the object feels too close, place it farther away until it's far enough for you to relax. It's important to create distance because breech feelings can trigger a part of you that's much younger and may feel helpless in the situation. You'll know when you've regained enough space between yourself and the situation because your body will feel more comfortable and you'll regain a sense of adulthood.

From your distanced, grown-up point of view, give yourself advice about what to do in that situation. If you're not sure what kind of advice to give yourself, ask a wise guide (ancestral or spiritual, or a role model) to join you and offer you advice. Your adult self and wise guide will never ask you to do anything rash or harmful and good advice will always make your physical symptoms improve. Proceed gently with yourself and your situation. Repeat this exercise until your kinesthetic sense of self feels balanced in the situation you've been working on.

NOTES

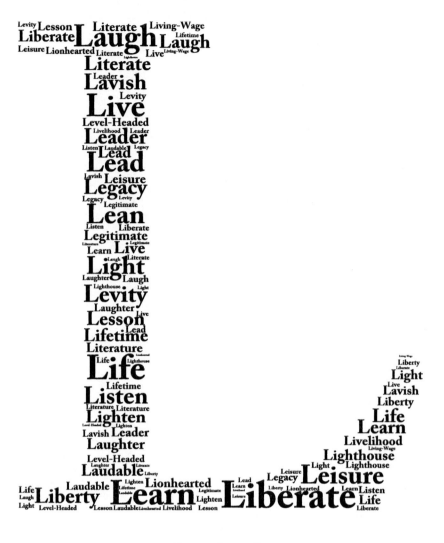

Lucky L

Laudable, Laugh, Laughter, Lavish, Lead, Leader, Lean, Learn,
Learned, Legacy, Legitimate, Leisure, Lesson, Level-headed,
Levity, Liberate, Liberation, Liberty, Life, Lifetime, Light, Lighten,
Lighthouse, Like, Lionhearted, Listen, Literate, Literature, Live,
Livelihood, Living, Living Wage, Longevity, Lounge, Love, Lovely,
Lover, Loyal, Loyalty, Luck, Lucky, Lucid, Luminary, Luminiferous,
Luminous, Luscious, Luster, Lustrous, Luxury, Lyric

ADD YOUR OWN GOLDEN L WORDS

_____

_____

_____

_____

_____

LAUDABLE: Deserving of praise

LAUGH: To make sounds of joy

LAUGHTER: A bodily sound that expresses joy

LAVISH: Abundant; luxurious

LEAD: To guide others

LEADER: Someone in the forefront who guides people

LEAN: Rest against something or someone for assistance
    or support

LEARN: To acquire knowledge or skills based on study
    or experience

LEARNED: Having a deep level of scholarly knowledge

LEGACY: A gift given from an ancestor, such as personal
    property, property, or money

LEGITIMATE: Authentic

LEISURE: Free time

LESSON: Instruction given; something learned

LEVEL-HEADED: Sensible

LEVITY: Lightness

LIBERATE: To free

LIBERATION: Freedom

LIBERTY: Freedom

LIFE: The experience of being alive; existence

LIFETIME: The time during which a person is alive

LIGHT: Illumination; carefree; the animating spirit in each person

LIGHTEN: To ease, for example, a burden

LIGHTHOUSE: A tall structure with a light on top intended to guide boats/ships

LIKE: Enjoy, prefer

LIONHEARTED: Brave, courageous

LISTEN: To give one's attention

LITERATE: A person who can read and write; a person who is educated

LITERATURE: Works of writing

LIVE: To be alive

LIVELIHOOD: The way a person makes a living to support him or herself

LIVING: Alive

LIVING WAGE: The amount of earnings needed for basic living conditions

LONGEVITY: Living a long life

LOUNGE: To relax

LOVE: Intense affection

LOVELY: Beautiful

LOVER: Someone who has deep affection for another person

LOYAL: Faithful

LOYALTY: Devotion

LUCK: Good fortune, blessing

LUCKY: Fortunate

LUCID: Clear

LUMINARY: A source of light from an object; a noteworthy person

LUMINIFEROUS: Generating light
LUMINOUS: Giving off light, illuminated
LUSCIOUS: Delicious
LUSTER: Soft light; sheen
LUSTROUS: Brilliant, radiant
LUXURY: Physical comfort
LYRIC: Exuberant

WRITE YOUR FAVORITE GOLDEN L WORDS HERE

_____

_____

_____

_____

_____

NOW USE YOUR FAVORITE GOLDEN L WORDS
TO CREATE YOUR OWN MANTRA OR AFFIRMATION

_____

_____

_____

_____

_____

Tool: Love the Unloved

Mother Teresa was widely known as a living saint because of her unconditional care for what many consider to be the most "untouchable" people, including those with leprosy, HIV/AIDS, and tuberculosis. She loved the "unloved." That kind of unconditional, open-hearted love is something that many people aspire to, but feel is beyond their ability. But you don't have to be a Mother Teresa to spread your love to the unloved.

Just imagine someone in your life who's difficult to love. Maybe it's someone else; maybe it's you. That person may be the person who needs love the most. Think about that person for a few minutes and ask yourself why he or she behaves or speaks in ways that annoy you. What is that person looking for? Maybe love, in his or her own way.

Imagine for a moment that you're Mother Teresa, an embodiment of unconditional love. Send out a ray of care and concern for that person. If that person is you, send a ray of love to yourself. There's nothing more to do, though if you want to take action, consider carefully. You can't control other people's reactions to your care, concern, love, and positive intentions. Unconditional means just that—you have no investment in the outcome. Just send love to this person on a regular basis. Observe what happens to your relationship.

Even Mother Teresa was human and criticized by those who like to find flaws. We're each doing our best at loving and receiving love. Give yourself credit for making an effort and give credit to others as well.

NOTES

_____

_____

_____

Magnificent M

Magic, Magical, Magnanimous, Magnificent, Maintain, Majestic,
Major, Make, Make-believe, Make-peace, Man, Manage, Mandala,
Manifest, Manipura, Manner, Mantle, Mantra, Manufacture, Manuscript,
Map, Marriage, Marvel, Marvelous, Massage, Master, Master Key,
Match, Maternal, Matter, Mature, Maverick, Maxim, May, Mazel Tov,
Meal, Meaning, Meaningful, Medal, Mediate, Medicine, Medicine
Man, Meditate, Meet, Mellow, Melody, Melt, Memento, Memoir,

Memorabilia, Memorable, Memorize, Memory, Mend, Mensch, Merchant, Mercy, Merit, Meritorious, Merry, Mesmerize, Message, Messenger, Metabolism, Metamorphosis, Metaphor, Method, Microphone, Mighty, Migrate, Mild, Millionaire, Mind, Mindful, Mine, Minister, Minstrel, Miracle, Mirror, Mirth, Mission, Mitzvah, Modest, Modulate, Money, Monument, Mood, Moral, Morale, More, Morning, Mosaic, Mother, Motherly, Motivate, Mountain, Mourn, Move, Movement, Moving, Muladhara, Munificent, Muse, Museum, Music, Mutual, Mystical, Myth, Mythological

ADD YOUR OWN GOLDEN **M** WORDS

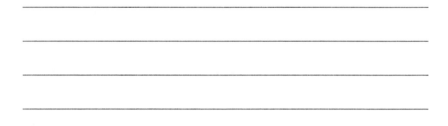

MAGIC: Supernatural or mysterious forces used to make things happen

MAGICAL: Captivating, enchanting, magnetic

MAGNANIMOUS: Generous, gracious, forgiving; noble of heart and mind

MAGNIFICENT: Outstanding

MAINTAIN: To keep something in working order; sustain

MAJESTIC: Dignified, royal, grand

MAJOR: Of key importance

MAKE: Create, construct, form

MAKE-BELIEVE: Intentionally suspend reality

MAKE-PEACE: A peacemaker

MAN: A male human being

MANAGE: To administer

MANDALA: A geometric symbol that represents unity

MANIFEST: To reveal or make plain

MANIPURA: The solar plexus chakra, which corresponds to will, purpose, and integrity

MANNER: The way in which something is done

MANTLE: A cloak

MANTRA: A sacred word or phrase that embodies and invokes divinity

MANUFACTURE: To create, build, or produce through a process

MANUSCRIPT: A written composition

MAP: To plan; to explore

MARRIAGE: A union

MARVEL: A genius; to be filled with amazement, wonder

MARVELOUS: Miraculous; causing astonishment

MASSAGE: Rubbing the body to bring relaxation

MASTER: A scholar; a person who is highly skilled

MASTER KEY: A key that opens many locks

MATCH: Two people or things that harmonize well together

MATERNAL: Motherly

MATTER: Something of importance; formless substance of the universe

MATURE: Fully developed physically, emotionally, conceptually

MAVERICK: An independent thinker

MAXIM: A proverb

MAY: A possibility

MAZEL TOV: Congratulations

MEAL: Food eaten at a routine time

MEANING: The inner importance; what something represents

MEANINGFUL: Full of significance

MEDAL: An object given as an award or honor

MEDIATE: Negotiate to resolve differences

MEDICINE: A remedy to treat a disease

MEDICINE MAN: A healer

MEDITATE: To contemplate or reflect, especially on a religious, devotional, or philosophical subject

MEET: To be introduced to someone; to get together

MELLOW: Soft, wise, smooth, mature

MELODY: A musical structure composed of a sequence of notes in a specific rhythm

MELT: To dissolve from solid to liquid; to relax; to disappear

MEMENTO: A special keepsake that reminds one of the past

MEMOIR: An autobiography that synthesizes a person's life experiences

MEMORABILIA: An object that is worthy of remembering

MEMORABLE: An experience or person that is worth remembering

MEMORIZE: To learn something by heart

MEMORY: Something that happened that is remembered; a recollection

MEND: To repair or correct

MENSCH: A person of integrity with commendable characteristics

MERCHANT: A shopkeeper

MERCY: Offering kind treatment

MERIT: Of value, worth

MERITORIOUS: Deserving of praise

MERRY: Festive, lively

MESMERIZE: To hypnotize, to enthrall (From physician F. A. Mesmer)

MESSAGE: A communication sent verbally or in written form

MESSENGER: One who brings a message, sometimes in reference to angels

METABOLISM: Processes in an organism needed to sustain life

METAMORPHOSIS: A transformation in form, personality, or other characteristic

METAPHOR: A figure of speech where a concept is used to designate another concept; an analogy

METHOD: A procedure developed to achieve something

MICROPHONE: A tool used to amplify the voice for speaking or singing

MIGHTY: Powerful

MIGRATE: To move from one place to another, usually to improve living circumstances

MILD: Gentle

MILLIONAIRE: A wealthy person

MIND: Intellect

MINDFUL: Attentive, thoughtful

MINE: A repository of something valuable

MINISTER: Attend to others' needs

MINSTREL: A traveling musician or poet

MIRACLE: A wondrous event that's not explicable by natural law

MIRROR: A reflection

MIRTH: Rejoicing and laughter often expressed in merrymaking

MISSION: A task that's been assigned either by oneself or another person/organization

MITZVAH: A good deed

MODEST: Reserved, humble

MODULATE: To adjust or adapt

MONEY: Currency used to purchase goods or services

MONUMENT: A structure of historical significance used to memorialize a person or event

MOOD: A state of mind, a feeling

MORAL: Ethical

MORALE: Confidence

MORE: Additional

MORNING: The beginning of the day

MOSAIC: Artwork created from small pieces of tile or glass

MOTHER: A woman who has given birth to a child; a female parent

MOTHERLY: Maternal; offering affection like a mother

MOTIVATE: To urge into action

MOUNTAIN: An element of the Earth's landscape with large height and mass

MOURN: Grieve

MOVE: To go from one place to another

MOVEMENT: Activity

MOVING: Emotionally touching

MULADHARA: The root chakra, located at the perineum, corresponds to survival, security, and vitality

MUNIFICENT: Generous

MUSE: To consider or ponder; the spirits watching over poets, artists, and musicians

MUSEUM: A place where valuable items are preserved

MUSIC: A melody created from instruments or voices

MUTUAL: Shared, in common

MYSTICAL: Beyond understanding due to its divine nature

MYTH: A story that is sometimes used to explain something

MYTHOLOGICAL: Fabulous, legendary

WRITE YOUR FAVORITE GOLDEN **M** WORDS HERE

_____

_____

_____

_____

_____

NOW USE YOUR FAVORITE GOLDEN M WORDS
TO CREATE YOUR OWN MANTRA OR AFFIRMATION

_____

_____

_____

_____

_____

Tool: Marvelous Mentors

Have you had mentors whose support, advice, recommendations, money, and other assistance gave you a much-needed boost to get into school, obtain a job, succeed at your work, acquire leadership opportunities, or complete a big project? A mentor can make the difference between success and failure. A mentor can advance you to the next level. Once you get there, it's your turn to be a mentor. The qualities of a good mentor are worth contemplating, then cultivating in ourselves.

Find a comfortable place to sit. Relax and close your eyes. Take a few slow, deep breaths in through your nose and out through your mouth or nose. Exhale out any stress or concerns. Then let your breathing become natural. Think about the qualities of one or more mentors. Did they see something in you that you hadn't even seen in yourself? Did they tell you a hard truth about something then help you improve? Did they open doors to exciting opportunities for you? What else did those mentors do for you?

Allow the flow of memories about your special mentor to come through you. As you consider these experiences, which words and qualities come to mind? Generous? Visionary? Ally? Strategic? Wise? Nurturing? Benefit of the doubt? Parental? Honest? Reliable? Forgiving?

Consider how you embody these qualities in yourself. How do you mentor others? How do you give to other people the gifts that were given to you? Which words that describe your mentor would you use to describe yourself? Are there qualities you'd like to embrace more fully?

Make a list of those qualities that your mentor embodies. Check off the ones that you practice. If there are qualities you'd like to embody more fully, decide how you'll go about living those qualities. If you feel inspired, write a letter of thanks to your mentor. That letter will be a treasure your mentor will cherish.

THE QUALITIES OF MY BEST MENTORS

_____

_____

_____

_____

_____

MENTOR QUALITIES I EMBODY

_____

_____

_____

_____

_____

Neutral N

Nail, Name, Nap, Narrate, Narrative, Nascent, Natal, Nation, Native, Natural, Nature, Naturopathy, Navigate, Neat, Necessary, Nectar, Negotiate, Neutral, New, New Year, Nice, Niche, Nifty, Night, Nimble, Nimbus, Nirvana, No, Noble, Noesis, Noon, Normal, Notable, Note, Nourish, Nourishment, Novel, Novice, Now, Nudge, Nugget, Numinous, Nurture, Nutrition, Nutritious

ADD YOUR OWN GOLDEN N WORDS

_____

_____

_____

_____

_____

Nail: To express or identify something exactly

Name: A word that identifies a person or thing

Nap: A brief sleep, usually outside the usual hours

Narrate: To tell an oral or written story

Narrative: An actual or fictional story

Nascent: Promising, emerging

Natal: Relating to birth

Nation: A group of people who live together in a country

Native: In a natural state

Natural: Found in nature

Nature: The physical world's natural scenery; the characteristics of a person or thing

Naturopathy: A branch of medicine that relies on natural remedies for healing

Navigate: To plan, write down, and follow a course of action to a destination

Neat: Orderly

Necessary: That which is needed to support existence, or meet a specific goal

Nectar: A delicious drink from the gods

NEGOTIATE: To reach an agreement on something in dispute

NEUTRAL: Unbiased, taking no sides in a dispute

NEW: Fresh; unfamiliar

NEW YEAR: The moment or day when the New Year begins; a fresh start

NICE: Pleasing, kind, virtuous

NICHE: A situation that fits well with a person's talents and personality

NIFTY: Well-designed, pleasing

NIGHT: The hours of darkness usually reserved for sleeping

NIMBLE: Agile, quick

NIMBUS: A positive aura about someone

NIRVANA: A state of bliss and freedom from the cares of the outer world

NO: Refusal

NOBLE: Upright character

NOESIS: Knowledge of universal forms

NOON: The brightest part or high point; zenith

NORMAL: Typical

NOTABLE: Remarkable, worthy of being noticed

NOTE: A short message of communication

NOURISH: To promote the development of something; to provide the substances needed for life and growth

NOURISHMENT: Food; fuel that supports life

NOVEL: New

NOVICE: A beginner

NOW: The present moment

NUDGE: To give a gentle push

NUGGET: A small, valuable item

NUMINOUS: Relating to the spiritual realm

NURTURE: To nourish and give sustenance

NUTRITION: Nourishment, food

NUTRITIOUS: Nourishing, healthful

WRITE YOUR FAVORITE GOLDEN **N** WORDS HERE

_____

_____

_____

_____

_____

NOW USE YOUR FAVORITE GOLDEN **N** WORDS TO CREATE YOUR OWN MANTRA OR AFFIRMATION

_____

_____

_____

_____

_____

Tool: Nourishing Naps

Remember when you were a child and had to take naps? Later on, you were old enough to skip the naps and go play instead. Finally, you grew up and got busy working long hours, raising a family, or involving yourself in important life goals. In the busy lives of most people, getting enough sleep, much less taking a nap, seems like a distant fantasy. Instead, in all our free time, most of us feel pressured to get more done.

But what if napping is the most important thing we can do? I'm not talking about constant couch-potato behavior. I'm referring to real rest when you're tired. You know when you're tired and you push through to your second wind? You think, "Oh phew, I got my second wind." But maybe to get there you grab a cup of coffee or other caffeinated drink. You realize you're not doing yourself any favors by pushing past tired to get more done. You don't need me to tell you that, but here I am, giving you that gentle reminder.

Sleep deficits and sleep irregularities pile up to bring on low grade, then chronic illness. Sleep is one of the most natural remedies you can give yourself. Our bodies know how to heal, but they need rest to recover. And did I mention it's free? So, next time you're tired, give in. Close your eyes and take an afternoon nap, or if it's nighttime, go to bed. You'll feel much more refreshed than if you push through to your second wind and try to catch up later. Turn off your phone before you close your eyes; there will be time for that once you're more rested. Even a catnap, 15 or 20 minutes of sleep, can bring benefits. So curl up like a cat (or a dog, if you prefer), and let go. If it turns into an hour, you must have needed it. Rest well and wake refreshed. You deserve it.

NOTES

Outstanding O

Oasis, Oath, Obligation, Observe, Obvious, Occupy, Ocean, Ode, Odyssey, Offer, Offset, Ointment, Old, Old-timer, Olive Branch, Olympian, Omen, One, Onward, Open, Open-hearted, Open-minded, Operate, Opportune, Opportunity, Optimism, Optimist, Optimum, Option, Opulent, Oracle, Orb, Orchestra, Orchestrate, Order, Ordinary, Ore, Organize, Orgasm, Orient, Origin, Original, Osculate, Outgoing,

Outlier, Outlive, Outreach, Outside, Outspoken, Outstanding, Overcome, Overhaul

ADD YOUR OWN GOLDEN O WORDS

_____

_____

_____

_____

_____

OASIS: A fertile area, with water and greenery, in the midst of a desert or other unpleasant place

OATH: A formal promise to fulfill a commitment

OBLIGATION: A legal commitment; indebted because of a special favor

OBSERVE: To pay attention, perceive, or notice

OBVIOUS: Apparent

OCCUPY: To take up space

OCEAN: A large body of salt water

ODE: An exalted poem

ODYSSEY: A long journey, a pilgrimage

OFFER: A proposal or suggestion

OFFSET: To balance

OINTMENT: A salve

OLD: Having lived or been around for a long time

Old-timer: Someone who has been around for a long time

Olive Branch: A peace offering

Olympian: A participant in the Olympic Games

Omen: A sign

One: Unity

Onward: Moving forward

Open: Accessible, available

Open-hearted: Kind, generous

Open-minded: Interested in new ideas

Operate: To work effectively

Opportune: Occurring at just the right moment

Opportunity: A favorable set of circumstances

Optimism: An inclination to expect the best outcome

Optimist: Someone who expects the best

Optimum: The best conditions in a specific situation

Option: A choice

Opulent: Abundant, prosperous, plentiful

Oracle: A source of prophetic wisdom

Orb: A sphere of influence

Orchestra: A group of musicians who play music together

Orchestrate: To arrange effectively

Order: To arrange methodically

Ordinary: Familiar

Ore: Valuable metal

Organize: To arrange in an orderly manner

Orgasm: Sexual climax

Orient: To get one's bearings

Origin: The source, beginning

Original: A new thing or idea; inventive, creative

Osculate: Kiss

Outgoing: Sociable

OUTLIER: Lying outside of the normal domain

OUTLIVE: To survive

OUTREACH: To reach beyond

OUTSIDE: The out-of-doors

OUTSPOKEN: Candid in speech

OUTSTANDING: Standing out from the rest due to excellence

OVERCOME: To prevail

OVERHAUL: To take apart for repairs

WRITE YOUR FAVORITE GOLDEN O WORDS HERE

_____

_____

_____

_____

_____

NOW USE YOUR FAVORITE GOLDEN O WORDS
TO CREATE YOUR OWN MANTRA OR AFFIRMATION

_____

_____

_____

_____

_____

Tool: One Word at a Time

Changing just one word can change the way you feel. Your mental focus and the meaning you attach to language determine your physical, emotional, mental, and spiritual states.

Your State of Mind

What is your personal mantra? If you always say to yourself, "I am stressed," you will find a host of reasons to support that feeling. But if you change that statement to, "I am relaxed," watch how your body and mind shift. Experiment for yourself right now. Say to yourself, "I am ... *stressed.*" Watch how your body and mind respond. Did you begin to make a list of everything you're stressing about? What was your physical reaction? Did your shoulders rise up? Did your belly or neck tighten? Did you get a knot in your throat? Now repeat the exercise, but substitute the word "relaxed" for "stressed." "I am ... *relaxed.*" Again, pay attention to the subtle shifts in your physical body and state of mind. Each time I practice this shift, I yawn into a state of relaxation. What are your physical cues for relaxing? Does your breath sink deeper into your belly? Does your chest loosen up? Do your shoulders relax down? Does your face go soft? Do your hips release?

Many people believe they need to feel stressed because of what's going on in their lives. However, a more relaxed state of mind will help you address your to-do list. In a stressed state, a to-do list can feel overwhelming. Being overwhelmed can lead you to try to get things done in a frenzy or make knee-jerk reactions. When you catch yourself feeling stressed, overwhelmed, or engaged in chaotic activity to get things done, stop and breathe in the feeling of the words "I am ... *relaxed*" until your body and mind make the shift. Then observe how that relaxed state allows your mind to naturally sort through your priorities and figure out what to do next. Taking a walk can serve a similar purpose because distracting your mind from stress breaks up your mental activity. You have the power to stop the old stream of thought and jump into a new stream.

You can also practice saying, "I am ... *relaxed*" while you're folding laundry, preparing dinner, or during any other routine where your mind is available. I like to practice this phrase while I clean vegetables for juicing. This is a repetitive task that takes about 15 minutes, but can feel like forever when I have so many other things to do. But what's the point of doing something healthy for yourself, like making juice, if the task is stressful and aggravating? So I get into a rhythm of washing, cutting, scrubbing, rinsing, and repeating this mantra, "I am ... *relaxed*." I feel better, solutions to problems I'd been worried about flow more naturally, and my reward is a big glass of fresh juice.

You can also substitute other words for "relaxed" like I am... *calm*. I am... *organized*. I am... *comfortable*. I am... *at ease*. I am... *doing something good for myself*. Changing one word can provide simple but dramatic shifts in your state of mind. In what parts of your life do you want to make a one-word shift? Choose a word from the 2,000+ golden words in this book and discover for yourself how one word can shift your state of mind.

Your Descriptive Words

This exercise can be done with other types of feeling statements in more complex situations. For example, let's say you feel rejected, which leads to the feeling of being unloved. You can say to yourself, "I am ... *unloved*." Or, you can say, "I was rejected, but I am *loved*" and allow your mind to search for those instances of feeling loved. This can be difficult where there's trauma. The mind may fight against the positive stream, but this is just the mind holding onto negativity because it thinks it's protecting you from further harm. Is it really? You may not feel loved by one person, and feeling loved doesn't erase that rejection, but you can avoid generalizing your feeling of being unloved by changing just one word. One rejection, after all, doesn't create a rule.

Here are some other "I am" statements you can say to yourself about yourself. These are not feeling states like *relaxed, calm,* and *comfortable;* instead they include descriptive words about positive, personal qualities. The opposite of these words will surely make you feel bad. Choose one you like and as you say it to yourself, observe the positive list your mind creates to support your "I am" statement. Enjoy the comforting and comfortable physical shifts that take place.

> I am ... beautiful.
> I am ... talented.
> I am ... a gift.
> I am ... kind.
> I am ... intelligent.
> I am ... gentle.
> I am ... confident.
> I am ... successful.
> I am ... easygoing.
> I am ... on time.
> I am ... (fill in the blank with a word you'd like to feel).

If your mind still fights against the statement, consider that you may have practiced a related negative statement for a long time or experienced a trauma so you aren't used to searching for evidence of the positive statement. Consider, too, that your habitual self-talk is often created based on adjectives and labels other people choose for you rather than those you choose for yourself. Choose adjectives to describe yourself that make you feel good. Keep practicing so you can cultivate those aspects of yourself.

Your Roles

There are many other words you can substitute in "I am" statements to make positive changes. For example, as you delve deeper into the roles you play in your life, you'll discover additional ways you identify yourself: according to your profession, your relationship to others, your philosophy, or your physical appearance.

PROFESSION: I am a _____
(Fill in the blank with your profession, e.g. real estate agent, coach, clothing designer, writer, teacher, editor, artist, actor, website designer, or whatever best fits you.)

RELATIONSHIP: I am a _____
(Fill in the blank with your roles, e.g. friend, mother, father, sister, brother, son, daughter, wife, husband, partner, lover, etc.)

PHILOSOPHY: I am a _____
(Fill in the blank with humanitarian, philanthropist, meditator, animal-rights activist, guardian of nature, etc.)

PHYSICAL APPEARANCE: I am a _____
(Fill in the blank with female, male, white, black, brown, short, tall, blonde, brown-eyed, etc.)

We all play many roles in our lives, but they aren't our true identity. We come into this world as spiritual beings, enter a body, live a life, then return to our original spirit states. Living a life gives us many choices. Sometimes we feel happy about our choices and sometimes we don't. At times, making a big change is what's needed to feel good in your skin, but before making big changes, see if you can make a shift in your basic state of mind by using the simpler statements in the above exercises. Once you create changes in your basic feeling state, your clarity of mind around your roles will improve. From that place of clarity, you'll feel more intuitively clear about the roles you want to live out in the world and whether you really need to change any of them.

If you decide to make a big change to any of your roles, consider what you'd rather do and create an "I am" statement to set yourself on course. Fully imagine yourself as that "I am" statement. How does it feel to "wear" a different "I am"? If you like the way it feels, consider the following in order to get yourself organized around the change:

- What adjustments need to be made to your life so you can make that *one word change* in your role? What steps and resources do you need to make this happen?
- Consider, with your own and others' best interests in mind, what you need to bring into your life and what you need to eliminate to make this one word change your reality.
- Sketch out a plan, do your research, make a vision board, and talk to people who can support your new "I am" role.

Repeat this exercise for any "I am" statement you'd like to shift. Be gentle with yourself as you make changes, especially big changes, which require a plan and a good support team.

Your True Self

Finally, we all want to be happy in our various roles, but at the core we're none of them. Our roles and physical appearance are like clothes we try on for dress-up games while we play here during our life. Letting go of what comes after the "I am," including the happy and relaxed statements, has the power to free us from the intensity of the game and enjoy the natural peace and happiness at our core for no other reason except that it's our true nature. When I had my near-death experience, I shed my roles along with my physical body, and experienced myself as pure spirit. As pure spirit, I felt content, at peace, and free. You can practice shedding your roles, identifications with your physical body, and attachments to certain feelings to discover your own pure spirit.

Find a comfortable place to sit and relax. Close your eyes and take a few deep, relaxing breaths. Now ask yourself, "Who am I?" As a description of yourself arises to answer the question, imagine shedding that role. Perhaps you wear certain clothes or have a particular persona in that role. Imagine setting it down next to yourself.

Ask yourself the same question again, "Who am I?" Again, as a description of yourself arises, set aside those associations and identifications next to you.

Continue with this line of questioning until you reach the end of your roles, identifications, feelings, and descriptions. Inside all these layers is your own pure spirit.

You can support your process with a visualization of literally setting aside those roles by putting them in a pile nearby, packing them into a trunk, or watching them dissolve like sugar crystals in a cup of water. As you clear away the layers of roles and labels you've taken on, imagine your bright spirit at the center waiting to be revealed. When you arrive, you will feel as if you've come home. That's the gift of knowing your pure spirit; you're always at home with yourself.

Persistent P

Pace, Pacific, Pacify, Pack, Package, Paean, Pair, Palace, Palatable, Palatial, Palliative, Pamper, Panorama, Paper, Papyrus, Parable, Parade, Paradigm, Paradise, Paradox, Paragon, Paramount, Paranormal, Parapsychology, Parchment, Pardon, Parent, Parity, Parole, Partake, Participate, Partner, Partnership, Party, Passable, Passage, Passenger, Passion, Pastoral, Patent, Paternal, Patience, Patient, Patriot, Pattern, Pay, Peace, Peaceful, Peacemaker,

Peace Offering, Peak, Pearl, Pedagogy, Pen, Pencil, Pendulum, Pension, Pensive, People, Pep, Perceive, Perceptive, Perfect, Perfectible, Perk, Perky, Permanent, Perseverance, Persevere, Persist, Persistent, Person, Personable, Personal, Personality, Perspective, Perspicacious, Perspicuous, Persuade, Pertinent, Pervade, Phenomenal, Phenomenon, Philanthropy, Philosopher, Philosopher's Stone, Philosophy, Photogenic, Photography, Photojournalism, Phototropism, Physiology, Physical Therapist, Physician, Picnic, Picture, Picturesque, Piety, Pilgrim, Pilgrimage, Pillar, Pillow, Pilot, Pioneer, Pious, Placable, Placate, Place, Placebo Effect, Placid, Plain, Plant, Play, Pleasant, Please, Pleasure, Pledge, Plenary, Plenitude, Plenteous, Plentiful, Plenty, Plethora, Pocket, Poem, Poet, Poetry, Poignant, Poise, Police, Policy, Polish, Polite, Ponder, Popular, Portend, Portent, Portfolio, Positive, Possession, Possibility, Possible, Post, Post-hypnotic, Posture, Potent, Potential, Pouch, Power, Powerful, Powwow, Practical, Practice, Practitioner, Pragmatic, Praise, Pray, Prayer, Precaution, Precious, Precipitation, Precise, Precocious, Precognition, Predict, Predominant, Preeminent, Pregnant, Premier, Premium, Prepare, Presage, Prescience, Prescient, Prescription, Presence, Present, Presentable, Presentiment, Preserve, Prestige, Presto, Pretend, Pretty, Prevail, Prevent, Primal, Primary, Prime, Principal, Principle, Print, Prismatic, Pristine, Private, Privilege, Prize, Pro, Proactive, Process, Proclaim, Procreate, Prodigious, Prodigy, Produce, Profession, Professional, Proficient, Profound, Prognosticate, Progress, Project, Promise, Prompt, Proof, Proper, Prophecy, Propose, Prosper, Prosperity, Protect, Proud, Prove, Proverb, Provide, Provision, Prowess, Prudent, Psalm, Psyche, Psychic, Psychokinesis, Public, Publicity, Publish, Puissant, Pulchritude, Pun, Punctual, Punctuate, Purchase, Pure, Purify, Purity, Purpose, Purposeful, Puzzle

ADD YOUR OWN GOLDEN P WORDS

_____

_____

_____

_____

_____

Pace: A set and achievable speed for an activity

Pacific: Calming

Pacify: To bring calm to a difficult situation

Pack: To collect items for travel

Package: A wrapped bundle of one or more items

Paean: An expression or song communicating joy

Pair: Two people who get together for a common purpose

Palace: A large ornate building used as a residence
   and fortress

Palatable: Agreeable to the senses and the taste buds

Palatial: Spacious and luxurious

Palliative: Something that soothes or alleviates pain

Pamper: To treat lavishly for relaxation

Panorama: The complete picture

Paper, Papyrus: Sheets made for writing

Parable: A story with a particular lesson or moral

Parade: A procession for a ceremonious occasion

Paradigm: A model or theory

Paradise: An ideal place or state of mind

Paradox: A contradiction that may in fact be true

PARAGON: A model of excellence

PARAMOUNT: Of foremost importance

PARANORMAL: Beyond the range of the five senses

PARAPSYCHOLOGY: The study of unexplained phenomena such as psychokinesis, telepathy, and clairvoyance

PARCHMENT: A surface made from an animal skin for writing or painting

PARDON: To forgive

PARENT: A father or mother; a guardian

PARITY: Equality

PAROLE: Release from prison for good behavior

PARTAKE: To share, participate

PARTICIPATE: To join in an activity with others

PARTNER: A mate or colleague joined together for a common purpose

PARTNERSHIP: Two or more people working together

PARTY: A get-together for enjoyment

PASSABLE: Able to move through

PASSAGE: Going from one place to another

PASSENGER: A traveler going from one place to another

PASSION: Intense enthusiasm; a strong emotion such as love or joy

PASTORAL: An idealization of rural life, such as a leisurely pace

PATENT: An inventor's exclusive right to produce, market, and sell an invention

PATERNAL: Fatherly, caring

PATIENCE: Able to wait and remain calm

PATIENT: Capable of calm during a time of waiting, delay, or annoyance

PATRIOT: Someone who loves their country

PATTERN: A design that's followed when creating something

Pay: Earnings in exchange for goods or services

Peace: Calm, serene, content

Peaceful: Tranquil

Peacemaker: Someone who assists those who are in dispute to come to an understanding

Peace Offering: An offering made to an opponent in an effort to reconcile

Peak: The summit or height of a mountain, an experience, or a positive emotion

Pearl: A prize; a lustrous gem created by an oyster in response to irritation (e.g., by a grain of sand)

Pedagogy: The art, science, and profession of teaching

Pen: A writing object filled with ink

Pencil: A writing/drawing tool made of wood with a cylinder of graphite

Pendulum: An object that swings back and forth to regulate a clock

Pension: Money paid out at and/or during retirement

Pensive: Thoughtfulness, contemplative

People: More than one person, usually a group

Pep: Lively, energetic

Perceive: To understand or become aware of; to notice

Perceptive: Keen, observant

Perfect: Whole, flawless, pure

Perfectible: Capable of perfection

Perk: A bonus, treat, or incentive

Perky: Alert, cheerful

Permanent: That which is enduring

Perseverance: Steadfastness

Persevere: Stay the course

Persist: To continue in an activity despite challenges

PERSISTENT: Enduring

PERSON: A human being

PERSONABLE: Agreeable in personality

PERSONAL: Private

PERSONALITY: The character and temperament of a person

PERSPECTIVE: A person's point of view

PERSPICACIOUS: Deeply insightful, wise

PERSPICUOUS: Expressed clearly and well understood

PERSUADE: To win someone over

PERTINENT: Relevant

PERVADE: To permeate

PHENOMENAL: Outstanding, remarkable

PHENOMENON: Something significant; a marvel

PHILANTHROPY: To support the well-being of humanity through charitable giving

PHILOSOPHER: A person who seeks truth and wisdom using the intellect

PHILOSOPHER'S STONE: A substance reputed to turn base metals into gold

PHILOSOPHY: Pursuit of wisdom and truth through rational means

PHOTOGENIC: Looking good in photos

PHOTOGRAPHY: The art of taking, processing, and printing photos

PHOTOJOURNALISM: Telling news stories with the use of photos

PHOTOTROPISM: A plant's movement toward the light as a growth response

PHYSIOLOGY: The essential life processes of an organism

PHYSICAL THERAPIST: A person licensed to help people improve strength and movement

PHYSICIAN: A person with a license to practice medicine

PICNIC: Something easy

Picture: A visual image

Picturesque: Scenic

Piety: Devotion

Pilgrim: A person who embarks on a sacred journey

Pilgrimage: A sacred journey

Pillar: A person who takes responsibility

Pillow: A cushion for resting one's head

Pilot: One who steers the course

Pioneer: An innovator; someone who explores the unknown

Pious: Devout, reverent

Placable: Easily calmed

Placate: To calm

Place: An area with specific boundaries

Placebo Effect: Medical benefit from an inactive substance that patients believe is medicinal

Placid: Remaining undisturbed, composed

Plain: Simple, clear

Plant: A vegetable, bush, or shrub that grows in the earth

Play: Recreation, enjoyable activity

Pleasant: Lovely, bringing pleasure

Please: Bring delight

Pleasure: Enjoyment

Pledge: Solemn promise

Plenary: Full, complete

Plenitude: Completeness, fullness

Plenteous: Abundant, copious

Plentiful: Abundant

Plenty: Full, adequate

Plethora: Superabundance

Pocket: A pouch sewed into a piece of clothing for carrying small items

POEM: Verse incorporating imagery and beautiful language meant to evoke feeling

POET: One who writes poems, poetry

POETRY: A form of literature incorporating beautiful and rhythmic language

POIGNANT: Emotionally moving

POISE: Ability to maintain balance, equilibrium

POLICE: An officer charged with protection of a community's citizens

POLICY: A contract outlining procedures

POLISH: To shine, refine, make smooth

POLITE: Good manners

PONDER: To meditate on something carefully

POPULAR: Well-liked

PORTEND: To foretell, foreshadow

PORTENT: Prophetic, omen

PORTFOLIO: A collection of items representing one's best work; investments

POSITIVE: Confident, accepting

POSSESSION: Items belonging to a person

POSSIBILITY: An opportunity or prospect

POSSIBLE: Capable of happening, achievable

POST: A letter

POST-HYPNOTIC: A suggestion given for an action or feeling to occur after hypnosis

POSTURE: How a person carries himself

POTENT: Powerful, effective

POTENTIAL: Possible, likely

POUCH: A small bag for carrying things

POWER: The strength for carrying out an activity effectively

POWERFUL: Influential

Powwow: A gathering where prayer occurs

Practical: That which is done in practice
as opposed to theory

Practice: To do something repeatedly in order to improve

Practitioner: Someone who practices a profession

Pragmatic: Practical; looking to facts and
historic events for outcomes

Praise: Compliment

Pray: In praise or petition of a higher power

Prayer: A petition for help from a higher power

Precaution: Caution against a possible danger

Precious: That which is beloved, cherished

Precipitation: Rain or snow

Precise: Exact, clear

Precocious: Advanced development

Precognition: Knowing in advance that something will happen

Predict: Foreknowledge

Predominant: Influential

Preeminent: Of major importance, outstanding, distinguished

Pregnant: Carrying a child; creative

Premier: First

Premium: A prize; first-class

Prepare: Get ready in advance

Presage: To know intuitively in advance

Prescience: Foresight, foreknowledge

Prescient: Having foreknowledge of an occurrence

Prescription: Medicine prescribed by a doctor

Presence: Being present

Present: A gift

Presentable: Able to be presented; fit for presentation

Presentiment: Premonition

Preserve: To protect from harm or spoilage

Prestige: Status earned via success

Presto: At once

Pretend: To make-believe

Pretty: Attractive

Prevail: To overcome, succeed, win

Prevent: To stop something from happening

Primal: Original

Primary: Fundamental

Prime: First in quality

Principal: Of primary importance

Principle: A truth

Print: Art of words on paper

Prismatic: Many-faceted; multicolored

Pristine: Pure; in its original state

Private: Kept away from the public

Privilege: Permission

Prize: Winnings, an award

Pro: A professional

Proactive: Taking the initiative

Process: A sequence of actions taken

Proclaim: To announce publicly

Procreate: To create offspring

Prodigious: Extraordinary, phenomenal, enormous

Prodigy: A person with an extraordinary gift or talent

Produce: Fruit and vegetables; create

Profession: The particular field a person chooses to work in

Professional: Someone engaged in their profession

Proficient: Perform adeptly

Profound: Deep

Prognosticate: To predict, using clues to guide

Progress: Advancement toward an objective

Project: A task

Promise: A vow to do something

Prompt: On time

Proof: Evidence

Proper: Appropriate

Prophecy: A prediction of the future

Propose: Suggest, recommend

Prosper: To thrive

Prosperity: Good fortune

Protect: To keep safe

Proud: Feeling delighted about an accomplishment

Prove: Demonstrate the truth of something

Proverb: A saying that expresses a widely accepted truth

Provide: To supply with what is needed

Provision: Necessary supplies

Prowess: Expertise

Prudent: Using good judgment, common sense

Psalm: A hymn

Psyche: The soul

Psychic: Pertaining to perception beyond the five senses

Psychokinesis: The ability to move objects
    with one's psychic powers

Public: The community

Publicity: Information shared about an event, a person,
    or a product

Publish: To prepare, print, and distribute written materials

Puissant: Mighty

Pulchritude: Physical beauty

Pun: A witty play on words

Punctual: On time, prompt

Punctuate: Use of punctuation marks

Purchase: To buy in exchange for money, goods, or services

Pure: Clean, unblemished

Purify: To clean

Purity: Innocence

Purpose: Goal, intention

Purposeful: Determined

Puzzle: A game of putting pieces together

WRITE YOUR FAVORITE GOLDEN P WORDS HERE

_____

_____

_____

_____

_____

NOW USE YOUR FAVORITE GOLDEN P WORDS TO CREATE YOUR OWN MANTRA OR AFFIRMATION

_____

_____

_____

_____

_____

Tool: Pretend Your Way to Real

Children have something on adults. They love pretending. They pretend to be adults in Mom's high heels or Dad's big shoes. They pretend to be teachers, lawyers, parents, singers, musicians, speakers, comics, chefs, and so on. Kids pretend in order to internalize what they see about growing up. They prepare for their adult lives through imitation and play.

Most of us stop pretending at some point in our lives. We decide that pretending is an avoidance of reality. Pretend play, after all, is for kids. "Grow up," people say. In fact, when we give up pretending, we freeze our current reality. Pretending opens up opportunities to experiment, learn, and grow—it is a kind of play that we may give up too soon.

If you think "pretending" is childish and scorn the idea of make-believe, consider that in hypnosis one way of bypassing the critical, conscious mind—in order to shift our mental/physical/emotional states—is through pretending and imagining.

Practice pretending, then follow up by doing the work to make your dream a reality, and soon you'll become what you've been pretending to be. I'm not saying it's always easy, but it's fun. It's child's play—and you know how to do it because you did it naturally as a child. Set time aside each day for daydreaming, pretending, and dressing the part.

NOTES

_____

_____

_____

_____

_____

Quality Q

Quaff, Qualified, Quality, Quantum, Quest, Question,
Quick, Quicken, Quiddity, Quiet, Quintessence

ADD YOUR OWN GOLDEN Q WORDS

_____

_____

_____

_____

_____

QUAFF: A hearty drink

QUALIFIED: Meeting specific requirements, competent

QUALITY: The feature of something

QUANTUM: Significant; the smallest unit of energy

QUEST: To seek, search

QUESTION: To inquire

QUICK: Bright, perceptive; speedy

QUICKEN: Vitalize; accelerate

QUIDDITY: The essence of something

QUIET: Calm, soothing, tranquil

QUINTESSENCE: The purest essence of something

WRITE YOUR FAVORITE GOLDEN Q WORDS HERE

_____

_____

_____

_____

_____

NOW USE YOUR FAVORITE GOLDEN Q WORDS
TO CREATE YOUR OWN MANTRA OR AFFIRMATION

_____

_____

_____

_____

_____

Tool: No Quitting?

Quitting may seem like an odd subject in a book about positive words, but sometimes we dedicate time and energy to something for a long time with few perceptible results. What then? When is the right time to quit and when is the right time to redirect or redouble our efforts?

When my nephew was a child, I brought him an educational kit that demonstrated how electricity works. We set up all the circuits, but the kit was poorly made and wouldn't complete the circuit without one of us holding everything in place, which was awkward and annoying. After some time, he finally tilted his head toward me, raised his eyebrows, and said, "No quitting allowed?" We'd taught him well.

I considered the situation and decided, in this case, quitting was not only allowed, but appropriate. It was time to move on to something more enjoyable and productive. The kit had to be returned; the principles of electricity taught some other time in some other way. We didn't give up on learning about electricity, but we quit that kit!

Is there something in your life that you've tried your best to accomplish or understand, but instead you're banging your head against the wall? Is it time to quit that approach and find a new way? Consider that quitting an approach that fails may open up solutions you hadn't considered before. The kit may need to be returned to make room for a better one.

NOTES

Resilient R

Radiance, Radiant, Radiate, Radio, Radiology, Rah, Rain, Rainbow, Rain Check, Raise, Rally, Range, Rapport, Rapt, Rapture, Rapturous, Rare, Rational, Rationale, Rave, Ray, Read, Reading, Reader, Ready, Real, Reality, Realization, Realize, Reap, Reason, Reasonable, Reassure, Rebate, Rebound, Receive, Receiver, Reception, Receptive, Recess, Recipe, Recipience, Recipient, Reciprocal, Reciprocate, Reciprocity, Reclaim, Recline, Recognition, Recognize, Recollect,

Recommend, Recommendation, Recommit, Recompense, Recompose,
Reconcilable, Reconcile, Reconsider, Reconstruct, Reconstruction,
Record, Recoup, Recover, Recovery, Recreate, Recreation, Recruit,
Rectify, Rectitude, Recuperate, Redeem, Redevelop, Redistribute,
Redouble, Reduce, Reeducate, Refill, Refine, Refit, Reflect, Reflective,
Reform, Refrain, Refresh, Refuge, Refund, Refuse, Refute, Regain,
Regal, Regale, Regard, Regenerate, Regimen, Regress, Regret,
Regular, Regulate, Rehearse, Reimburse, Reinvest, Rejoice, Rejoin,
Rejuvenate, Relate, Relation, Relationship, Relax, Release, Relevant,
Relief, Relieve, Relish, Relume, Remain, Remake, Remarkable,
Remedy, Remember, Remembrance, Remind, Reminisce, Remission,
Remittance, Remodel, Remorse, Remove, Remunerate, Renascent,
Renegotiate, Renew, Renovate, Renown, Repair, Reparation, Repast,
Repent, Replant, Replenish, Replete, Repose, Reprieve, Reproduce,
Reputable, Rescue, Research, Reserve, Reservoir, Reside, Resilience,
Resilient, Resolute, Resolution, Resolve, Resonance, Resonant,
Resonate, Resound, Respect, Respire, Respite, Resplendent, Respond,
Responsible, Responsive, Rest, Restitution, Restorative, Restore,
Result, Resurrect, Resuscitate, Retire, Retirement, Retouch, Retreat,
Retrieve, Return, Reunion, Reunite, Reveal, Revel, Revelation,
Revenue, Revere, Reverent, Reverie, Revise, Revision, Revive,
Revivify, Revolution, Revolutionary, Reward, Rhapsody, Rhyme,
Rhythm, Rich, Right, Rigorous, Ripe, Rise, Risibility, Risk, Ritual,
River, Rivet, Road, Roar, Robust, Rock, Rocker, Rocket, Romance,
Romantic, Roomy, Roots, Roses, Rouse, Royal, Run, Rustic

ADD YOUR OWN GOLDEN R WORDS

_____

_____

RADIANCE: Glow, warmth

RADIANT: Giving off light or heat, bright, glowing

RADIATE: To give off a glow

RADIO: Use of electromagnetic waves to send communications such as music or speaking

RADIOLOGY: Use of X-ray radiation for medical diagnosis

RAH: An abbreviation for the cheer "hurrah"

RAIN: Abundant giving; water falling to the earth from rainclouds

RAINBOW: An arc of multicolored, spectral light that often appears in the sky after a rain

RAIN CHECK: A promise to make good on a postponed or sold out offer

RAISE: To promote one's position or pay; to rear, nurture

RALLY: To meet for a collective purpose; to revive one's strength

RANGE: The scope of ability, experience, or knowledge

RAPPORT: A relationship of trust, affinity, and connection

RAPT: Captivated, engrossed

RAPTURE: An ecstatic state

RAPTUROUS: Filled with ecstasy

RARE: Unusual

RATIONAL: Reasonable, lucid, coherent

RATIONALE: The reasons for something

RAVE: Extreme enthusiasm

RAY: A beam of light

READ: To understand the written word

READING: The act of engaging with printed material

READER: Someone who can read

READY: Prepared

REAL: Authentic, genuine, true

REALITY: A true situation that actually exists

REALIZATION: Insight; achievement

REALIZE: To understand completely; to attain something

REAP: To harvest

REASON: The basis for an action or decision

REASONABLE: Rational, sensible

REASSURE: To comfort or put at ease

REBATE: To deduct or refund a portion of payment

REBOUND: To spring back after a disappointment

RECEIVE: To take something that was given

RECEIVER: Someone who receives

RECEPTION: A welcome

RECEPTIVE: Open to receiving

RECESS: A break from work

RECIPE: A formula for mixing medicine, preparing food, or making another creation

RECIPIENCE: The capacity to receive

RECIPIENT: One who receives

RECIPROCAL: Mutual

RECIPROCATE: To engage in mutual giving and taking

RECIPROCITY: A mutual interchange in a relationship

RECLAIM: To convert wasteland in usable land; to take back

RECLINE: To lean back

RECOGNITION: An awareness of having seen something before

RECOGNIZE: To know; to acknowledge

RECOLLECT: To remember

RECOMMEND: To endorse someone as worthy

RECOMMENDATION: A favorable endorsement

RECOMMIT: To commit again

RECOMPENSE: To make amends; to pay for services

RECOMPOSE: To reorganize; to compose oneself again

RECONCILABLE: Capable of reconciliation

RECONCILE: To settle a disagreement

RECONSIDER: To consider again

RECONSTRUCT: To rebuild, renovate

RECONSTRUCTION: Rebuilding

RECORD: To preserve information, usually in written form; music preserved in one form or another

RECOUP: To recover something that was lost in an equivalent form

RECOVER: To restore

RECOVERY: Return to normal

RECREATE: To refresh oneself mentally and physically

RECREATION: Relaxation; the enjoyment of pleasurable activities

RECRUIT: To enroll someone as an ally

RECTIFY: To make something right

RECTITUDE: Moral decency

RECUPERATE: To recover one's health

REDEEM: To restore as in one's reputation; to turn in for cash or other item

REDEVELOP: To revitalize an area that's rundown

REDISTRIBUTE: To change the distribution of something

REDOUBLE: To intensify, repeat

REDUCE: To lower the quantity of something

REEDUCATE: To educate again to be more effective, rehabilitate

REFILL: To fill again

REFINE: To purify; polish, improve

REFIT: To repair, overhaul

REFLECT: To consider; to mirror

REFLECTIVE: Thoughtful

REFORM: To alter or change for the better

REFRAIN: To hold back

REFRESH: To renew, rejuvenate, revive

REFUGE: A safe place, shelter, or sanctuary

REFUND: To give back something that was paid

REFUSE: To decline

REFUTE: To show an argument or statement is incorrect

REGAIN: To recover

REGAL: Magnificent

REGALE: To entertain

REGARD: To show admiration or respect

REGENERATE: To renew or replace

REGIMEN: A systematic approach to treatment

REGRESS: Return to an earlier time

REGRET: To grieve a loss or disappointment

REGULAR: The usual, normal

REGULATE: To set up for accurate functioning

REHEARSE: To prepare

REIMBURSE: Repay, compensate

REINVEST: To invest again

REJOICE: To celebrate with joy

REJOIN: To join again in company

REJUVENATE: Revitalize, renew

RELATE: To tell; to interact meaningfully

RELATION: People connected by marriage or blood

RELATIONSHIP: A bond of friendship, marriage, or blood

RELAX: To be at ease, loosen up

RELEASE: To liberate, to let go

RELEVANT: Pertinent to the matter

RELIEF: Release from something challenging, aid

RELIEVE: Alleviate something difficult

RELISH: To enjoy, take delight in

RELUME: To re-illuminate

REMAIN: To stay

REMAKE: To make something again, reconstruct

REMARKABLE: Extraordinary

REMEDY: A medicine or therapeutic approach

REMEMBER: To recall a memory, think of again

REMEMBRANCE: Something serving to commemorate a person or event

REMIND: To bring something back to mind

REMINISCE: To recollect the past

REMISSION: To release from something

REMITTANCE: Payment

REMODEL: To reconstruct, renovate

REMORSE: Regret

REMOVE: To take something away

REMUNERATE: To pay someone for goods or services

RENASCENT: Come back to life; reviving

RENEGOTIATE: To revise terms of a previous agreement

RENEW: To restore, make new again

RENOVATE: To improve the condition

RENOWN: Fame and respect

REPAIR: To fix

REPARATION: The act of making amends

REPAST: A meal

REPENT: To feel sorry for something you've done

REPLANT: To plant again

REPLENISH: To fill up again

REPLETE: A bountiful supply

REPOSE: Rest

REPRIEVE: Acquittal

Reproduce: Procreate

Reputable: Trustworthy, respectable

Rescue: Save

Research: Investigation, inquiry

Reserve: To keep for future use

Reservoir: A large lake or pool for storing water

Reside: To live in a place permanently or for a long time

Resilience: The ability to recover quickly

Resilient: Able to recover quickly, strong

Resolute: Showing determination in pursuit of a purpose

Resolution: Firm determination; decision

Resolve: To find an answer; to be firm in a decision

Resonance: To find personally significant

Resonant: Deeply affecting a person

Resonate: To sound or feel familiar

Resound: To fill with sound

Respect: To treat with consideration, to honor

Respire: To breathe

Respite: A pause during a time of discomfort that offers relief

Resplendent: Brilliant, dazzling

Respond: To give an answer or reply

Responsible: Accountable, upholding one's obligations

Responsive: Readily responding

Rest: Peace, tranquility; break from work

Restitution: Restoring something to its rightful owner

Restorative: Renewing, especially in regard to health

Restore: Bring back to a normal condition

Result: Consequence

Resurrect: Bring back to life

Resuscitate: To revive, bring back to consciousness

Retire: To depart for rest

RETIREMENT: Retreat; leaving a career or job

RETOUCH: To add details for improvement

RETREAT: A period of solitude

RETRIEVE: To get something back, restore

RETURN: To go back to a place or a condition

REUNION: Coming together after a separation

REUNITE: To come back together

REVEAL: To uncover, show

REVEL: Rejoice

REVELATION: Disclosure of the divine

REVENUE: Income

REVERE: To show respect, veneration

REVERENT: Feeling respect, awe

REVERIE: Daydream

REVISE: To make changes; to rethink

REVISION: An altered version of something

REVIVE: To breathe life into again, resuscitate

REVIVIFY: Rejuvenate

REVOLUTION: Dramatic change

REVOLUTIONARY: Bringing about groundbreaking change

REWARD: Compensation or gift

RHAPSODY: Enthusiasm and joy expressed in speech or writing

RHYME: A poem whose lines end with words with the same ending sounds

RHYTHM: Regularity of beat or tempo

RICH: Wealthy in something of great importance to the individual

RIGHT: Accurate; just

RIGOROUS: Thoroughly accurate

RIPE: Fully matured

RISE: To come up, to increase

RISIBILITY: Humorousness

RISK: The possibility of danger

RITUAL: A method that's often followed for prayer or ceremony

RIVER: A flowing body of water

RIVET: To engross

ROAD: An open passageway for going somewhere

ROAR: A loud noise, sometimes made in uproarious laughter

ROBUST: Hardy

ROCK: A solid mass either plain, precious, or semi-precious

ROCKER: A chair or device that rocks

ROCKET: A high velocity device capable of space travel

ROMANCE: A love affair

ROMANTIC: Inclined to express affection

ROOMY: Spacious

ROOTS: The underground part of a plant providing stability and nourishment; ancestry

ROSES: Easy situation

ROUSE: To wake from apathy

ROYAL: Majestic

RUN: Move quickly

RUSTIC: Simple, plain

WRITE YOUR FAVORITE GOLDEN R WORDS HERE

NOW USE YOUR FAVORITE GOLDEN **R** WORDS
TO CREATE YOUR OWN MANTRA OR AFFIRMATION

_____

_____

_____

_____

_____

Tool: Ride the River to Your Goal

We learn in grade school that the Earth is about 70 percent water. Despite this vast amount of flowing water, moving through life toward our heartfelt goals feels slow and sluggish at times. To shift from slow to an easier flow, take a gondola ride down the river.

Find a comfortable place to sit and relax. Think about a part of your life that feels sluggish or stopped up. Create an intention to bring flow to that aspect of your life. Bring yourself to the bank of a river. There's a gondola waiting there for you along with one or two of your most trusted friends or guides. Also waiting there is the most powerful, successful, and confident aspect of yourself. This might be a past, present, or future part of you. This aspect of you wants to accompany and encourage you.

Walk to the riverbank and imagine stepping into the beautiful carved gondola. The gondolier, the driver of this boat, takes your hand as you step aboard and find a comfortable, steady seat in the boat. Your guides step in along with the successful aspect of yourself.

As the gondolier begins to paddle down the river, imagine your heartfelt goal at the destination, which is straight ahead at the mouth of the river. The river is calm, and the gondolier's oars move through the water in a gentle rhythm. First the gondolier paddles on one side, then paddles on the other side. With each movement of the oar through the water, you feel more and more relaxed as you surrender to the easy flow of the gondola moving downstream with the current. Your breath falls into rhythm with the paddling of the oars.

At first, your attention may drift to the people and events along either shore. Some may be helpers, some may be distractions from your goal. Invite the helpers to walk along the riverbank and meet you at your destination. Allow the distractions to fall away as the gondola drifts with the current, drawing your attention more and more steadily to your goal at the mouth of the river. As you draw closer and closer to your goal, everything in your peripheral vision quiets down and fades away except what's helping you. Your goal ahead becomes like a bull's-eye at the center of a target. You begin to make out the details, some of which might surprise you and even give you additional ideas and inspiration for understanding and reaching your goal.

As you reach the mouth of the river, you see your dream come true and people there to greet you. The gondolier docks the boat and a special person reaches for your hand to help you disembark. You step onto dry land and walk about your living dream, taking in the sights, sounds, and smells with all your senses. You can feel it and take in the joy and celebration of the moment. You smile as you feel the contentment of reaching your goal.

When you're ready, open your eyes. Take notes on any part of the experience you'd like to remember. Take a gondola ride anytime you'd like to relax in the flow toward your accomplishment, assisted by the current of the river, your empowered self, your guides and resources, and your gondolier.

Sacred S

Sacred, Sacrosanct, Safe, Safeguard, Sagacious, Sage, Sahasrara, Saint, Salary, Sale, Saltant, Salubrious, Salutary, Salutation, Salute, Salvable, Salvage, Salvation, Salve, Sanctify, Sanctity, Sanctuary, Sanitary, Sanity, Satiable, Satiety, Satin, Satisfied, Satisfy, Save, Savior, Savor, Savory, Saying, Scenery, Scholar, Scholarly, Scholarship, Scholastic, School, Science, Scintillate,

Scrumptious, Scruple, Scrupulous, Scrutable, Scrutinize,
Scrutiny, Sea, Search, Seasoned, Secure, See, Seemly, Self,
Self-confidence, Self-contained, Self-defense, Self-determination,
Self-discipline, Self-educated, Self-esteem, Self-expression,
Self-improvement, Self-knowledge, Self-love, Self-mastery,
Self-preservation, Self-realization, Self-reliance, Self-respect,
Self-restraint, Self-starter, Self-sufficient, Self-support,
Self-sustaining, Self-taught, Seminar, Sensation, Sensibility,
Sensitive, Sensuous, Sentience, Sentient, Seraph, Serenade,
Serene, Serious, Serve, Service, Sex, Shade, Shakti, Shaman,
Share, Sheen, Shelter, Shield, Shimmer, Shine, Shower, Sight,
Sign, Signal, Significant, Silence, Silent, Silk, Silky, Simple,
Simplify, Sincere, Sing, Skeptical, Sky, Sleep, Slow, Smart,
Smile, Smooth, Snack, Snow, Snug, Snuggle, Soap, Soar,
Sobriquet, Sociable, Social, Society, Soft, Solace, Solar, Solid,
Solitude, Solution, Solvable, Soma, Somnifacient, Somniferous,
Somnolent, Song, Sonorous, Soothe, Sorry, Soul, Soulful, Sound,
Source, Spacious, Spare, Spark, Sparkle, Speak, Special, Specific,
Spectacular, Speech, Spend, Spice, Spirit, Spirited, Spiritous,
Spiritual, Splendent, Splendid, Splendiferous, Splendor,
Spontaneous, Sport, Spouse, Spring, Stable, Stalwart, Stamina,
Stand, Standard, Stand-up, Staple, Star, Start, Steadfast, Steady,
Stimulate, Story, Strategy, Strength, Strengthen, Strong, Strong-
minded, Structure, Study, Substantial, Subtle, Succeed, Success,
Successful, Succor, Sufficient, Suggestion, Summer, Summit,
Sun, Sunny, Sunrise, Super, Superabundant, Superb, Superlative,
Supplicate, Supply, Support, Sure, Surgery, Surmount, Surplus,
Surprise, Surrender, Survive, Sustain, Sustenance, Svadhisthana,
Svelte, Sweat, Sweet, Sweeten, Sweetheart, Swift, Swing,
Symbol, Symmetry, Sympathy, Symphony, Synthesize, System

ADD YOUR OWN GOLDEN S WORDS

_____

_____

_____

_____

_____

SACRED: Worthy of respect, reverence

SACROSANCT: Sacred, inviolable

SAFE: Protected from danger

SAFEGUARD: Preserve, defend

SAGACIOUS: Wise

SAGE: A wise person

SAHASRARA: The chakra of a thousand petals, located at the crown of the head, corresponds to Universal Consciousness

SAINT: A charitable, patient person; a holy person

SALARY: Pay for services

SALE: Specially discounted prices for goods or services

SALTANT: Dancing, leaping, or jumping

SALUBRIOUS: Healthful

SALUTARY: Beneficial

SALUTATION: An expression of goodwill or greeting

SALUTE: A welcome address

SALVABLE: Able to be saved

SALVAGE: To save

SALVATION: Saved from difficulty

Salve: A medicinal, soothing, healing ointment

Sanctify: To purify, make sacred

Sanctity: Sacredness

Sanctuary: A holy place; a safe haven, refuge

Sanitary: Clean

Sanity: Sound judgment; good mental health

Satiable: Able to be satisfied

Satiety: The quality of being full

Satin: Smooth, silky fabric

Satisfied: Content, gratified, fulfilled

Satisfy: To fulfill

Save: To bring to safety; rescue from danger;
    to put aside for later

Savior: Someone who saves another person; a protector

Savor: Deeply enjoy a flavor or experience

Savory: Flavorful

Saying: A wise saying or adage

Scenery: A landscape

Scholar: A learned person

Scholarly: Educated, knowledgeable

Scholarship: A grant for a student to attend a university

Scholastic: Academic

School: An institution of learning

Science: A method of study for acquiring knowledge

Scintillate: Sparkle

Scrumptious: Delectable

Scruple: Ethical consideration; conscience

Scrupulous: Principled

Scrutable: Comprehensible through study

Scrutinize: Study with care

Scrutiny: Careful study or examination

Sea: A large body of saltwater

Search: Explore

Seasoned: Competent

Secure: Safe

See: To observe with the eyes; to visualize, imagine

Seemly: Becoming

Self: The essential part of a person

Self-confidence: Confidence in oneself

Self-contained: Self-sufficient

Self-defense: The right to protect oneself

Self-determination: Freedom to choose one's own fate

Self-discipline: Self-control

Self-educated: Self-directed education of oneself

Self-esteem: Being aware of one's own worth and value

Self-expression: Expressing one's feelings and personality

Self-improvement: Self-effort for personal growth

Self-knowledge: Knowing oneself and one's abilities

Self-love: Regard for oneself

Self-mastery: Self-control

Self-preservation: The instinct to protect oneself from harm

Self-realization: Fulfillment of one's highest possibilities

Self-reliance: Capable of relying on one's judgment

Self-respect: Esteem for oneself

Self-restraint: Able to control oneself

Self-starter: Initiative

Self-sufficient: Able to take care of oneself

Self-support: Able to support oneself, especially financially

Self-sustaining: Able to maintain oneself independently

Self-taught: Teaching oneself without official instruction

Seminar: A small group meeting for pursuit in research or study

Sensation: Feeling coming from the five senses

SENSIBILITY: Keen perception

SENSITIVE: Highly perceptive

SENSUOUS: Appealing to the senses

SENTIENCE: Consciousness

SENTIENT: Able to experience sensation

SERAPH: An angelic being

SERENADE: A song by a sweetheart for his lover

SERENE: Tranquil

SERIOUS: Thoughtful, showing dedication

SERVE: To offer assistance

SERVICE: Helpful deed

SEX: Mating for pleasure and/or reproduction

SHADE: An area protected from sunlight

SHAKTI: Dynamic cosmic energy

SHAMAN: Medicine man

SHARE: A portion or idea given away

SHEEN: Shine

SHELTER: A refuge

SHIELD: Something worn or used for protection

SHIMMER: A flickering light, a glimmer

SHINE: Radiant, bright

SHOWER: An abundant outpouring; a brief rainfall

SIGHT: The faculty of eyesight

SIGN: Omen

SIGNAL: Remarkable

SIGNIFICANT: Meaningful

SILENCE: Complete quiet, stillness

SILENT: The state of being quiet and still

SILK: A lustrous fabric originating from silkworm fiber

SILKY: Lustrous, soft

SIMPLE: Straightforward, humble

SIMPLIFY: To make less elaborate

SINCERE: True, honest

SING: Putting words to a melody

SKEPTICAL: Questioning

SKY: The upper limit; the upper atmosphere

SLEEP: A period of rest

SLOW: Unhurried

SMART: Intelligent

SMILE: A happy expression where the corners of the mouth are turned up

SMOOTH: Even; serene

SNACK: A small meal

SNOW: White ice crystals falling from the sky

SNUG: Cozy

SNUGGLE: Sit close together, cuddle

SOAP: A liquid or solid cleanser

SOAR: Fly high; to be inspired

SOBRIQUET: An affectionate nickname

SOCIABLE: Friendly

SOCIAL: Sociable, communal

SOCIETY: Civilization

SOFT: Smooth to the touch; gentle

SOLACE: To comfort during a difficult time

SOLAR: Coming from the sun

SOLID: Well-made

SOLITUDE: Time alone, privacy

SOLUTION: An answer

SOLVABLE: Able to be solved

SOMA: The body

SOMNIFACIENT: Hypnotic

SOMNIFEROUS: Producing sleep

Somnolent: Sleepy

Song: Poetry or verse set to music

Sonorous: Impressive

Soothe: Comfort, calm down

Sorry: Expressing sympathy or apology

Soul: The animate or nonphysical aspect of a person

Soulful: Full of feeling

Sound: Valid; trustworthy

Source: The origin

Spacious: Roomy

Spare: To treat leniently

Spark: Glimmer, flash

Sparkle: Glitter, effervesce

Speak: Talk, express oneself

Special: Exceptional

Specific: Definite

Spectacular: Remarkable

Speech: The spoken word

Spend: Use money

Spice: Something used to add extra flavor

Spirit: The animating force in living things

Spirited: Courageous

Spiritous: Pure

Spiritual: Related to spirit, sacred, mystical

Splendent: Lustrous; celebrated

Splendid: Radiant

Splendiferous: Splendid, outstanding

Splendor: Magnificent, brilliant display

Spontaneous: Happening in the moment, unplanned

Sport: Diversion for recreational purposes

Spouse: Marriage partner

SPRING: A source of water; the beginning; the season when plants emerge, animals mate and nest, and the weather becomes milder

STABLE: Enduring

STALWART: Sturdy, resolute

STAMINA: Strength and endurance to resist illness, fatigue, or challenges

STAND: Upright

STANDARD: Measure of quality used to create a norm

STAND-UP: Durable, satisfactory

STAPLE: Essential

STAR: Our life-giving sun; a luminous mass

START: To begin

STEADFAST: Unwavering, loyal

STEADY: Reliable

STIMULATE: To motivate to action

STORY: The narrative relating to an event

STRATEGY: An action plan

STRENGTH: Emotional or physical power

STRENGTHEN: Make stronger

STRONG: Resilient, sturdy; healthy

STRONG-MINDED: Strong-willed

STRUCTURE: An organized pattern

STUDY: Pursuit and investigation of knowledge

SUBSTANTIAL: Real, solid, important

SUBTLE: Understated

SUCCEED: Prosper; thrive

SUCCESS: Achievement of an intended goal

SUCCESSFUL: Having a favorable result

SUCCOR: Relief during a distressful time

SUFFICIENT: Enough, adequate

SUGGESTION: An idea or recommendation

SUMMER: The warmest season of the year

SUMMIT: The height of achievement

SUN: The star of our solar system that enables life on Earth

SUNNY: Cheerful

SUNRISE: The time when our sun starts to become visible above the eastern horizon

SUPER: Fabulous

SUPERABUNDANT: More than enough

SUPERB: Outstanding

SUPERLATIVE: Unparalleled excellence

SUPPLICATE: To humbly pray

SUPPLY: Provisions

SUPPORT: To aid someone or a cause

SURE: Unwavering

SURGERY: Medical treatment for injury or illness that may be life-saving

SURMOUNT: To overcome, as in a challenge or obstacle

SURPLUS: Extra, left-over

SURPRISE: Unexpected amazement

SURRENDER: Let go

SURVIVE: To stay alive

SUSTAIN: To maintain existence

SUSTENANCE: Nourishment; livelihood

SVADHISTHANA: The navel chakra, which corresponds to creativity, pleasure, and relationships

SVELTE: Graceful

SWEAT: Perspiration released to cool the body and release toxins

SWEET: Lovable; pleasurable

SWEETEN: To improve

SWEETHEART: An affectionate term for a loved one

SWIFT: Fast

SWING: To rock

Symbol: Something that's used to represent something else

Symmetry: Beauty created through harmony and balance

Sympathy: Shared understanding with another;
   compassion for another's distress

Symphony: Harmonious and complex arrangement of elements,
   usually musical

Synthesize: To combine many elements into a new form

System: A group of interrelated elements forming a functional whole

WRITE YOUR FAVORITE GOLDEN S WORDS HERE

_____

_____

_____

_____

_____

NOW USE YOUR FAVORITE GOLDEN S WORDS
TO CREATE YOUR OWN MANTRA OR AFFIRMATION

_____

_____

_____

_____

_____

Tool: Soothing Silk Scarves

Shortly after my bike accident I developed a nervous system disorder that was eventually diagnosed as RSDS (reflex sympathetic dystrophy syndrome), now called CRPS (chronic regional pain syndrome). I had never experienced such severe, chronic pain and couldn't imagine how it would ever resolve. The happy ending is that the pain *did* resolve thanks to alternative medical approaches I found through diligent self-care, which brought me important leads from trusted doctors.

I also learned to relax and manage physical tension using self-hypnosis procedures including guided imagery and metaphors. The process I'm sharing here is not meant to replace treatment for chronic pain or to treat acute pain that requires a doctor's visit or a trip to the emergency room, but it can reduce discomfort and tension through daily practice. Used in concert with appropriate techniques developed for the individual client, alongside the support—if needed—of a good physical therapist, massage therapist, and other possible modalities, discomfort that no longer has a meaningful cause can be reduced significantly and even resolved.

When an injury is fresh and healing, we experience meaningful pain. Once the injury has healed, the pain ought to go away, too. Pain that continues when there's no longer an injury or pathology is no longer meaningful pain, but rather an internal feedback loop that needs to be interrupted.

I learned from working with doctors and physical therapists, reading the literature on RSDS, and studying medical hypnosis that when this feedback loop keeps playing, even though there are no more external messages coming in to trigger the pain, then new external information has to be introduced to normalize the nervous system and the pain response. This includes desensitizing massage, which can be difficult for a person in pain for whom being touched, wearing clothes, or even feeling a breeze is exquisitely distressing.

But even when an actual sensory experience creates discomfort, it's possible to introduce an imaginary sensory comfort. You can do this by using the sense memory of something you once enjoyed. In this tool, I'll be using the sensory experience of silk scarves. If you've never touched a piece of silk, you can imagine something else soft that you enjoy such as velvet, flannel, fleece, Egyptian cotton, or fur. The memory of petting a soft cat, dog, or other pet will work, too.

Make yourself comfortable either sitting or lying down. If there's a lot of tension in your body, take a moment just to breathe. Breathe in deeply, hold that breath for a few seconds, then release it out with your tension. Take another deep breath in, hold it for a few seconds, then let it carry away all your worries. Now let your breath be fluid, like water that's exactly the temperature you like, and easily permeate every cell of your body. As you breathe, imagine your chosen soft fabric in your hands. I'll use silk as my example. Draw your hands across this imaginary piece of silk. Rub it between your fingers. As you do so, watch as your breath continues to loosen up and the tension in your hands goes soft, like a silk scarf. As your hands go soft, allow that relaxation to travel up your arms to your shoulders. Allow your shoulders to relax down, if possible, and be as soft as a newborn baby.

Now imagine the silk scarf on your face, then gently wrapped around your neck. Allow the silk scarf to flow right into your skin, becoming one with your nerves, muscles, and brain. As your neck and face muscles turn into soft, silk scarves, keep rubbing the silk between your fingers. Allow the feeling of silk in your fingertips and neck to flow through your arms and go soft and loose, like silk scarves just sitting in a pile. Feel your hands and fingers open and collapse, like more silk scarves.

Now the silky scarves flow down from your head and neck into your chest, belly, and arms. Feel your breath relax deeply as all your insides unwind like a soft silk scarf, soothing as warm water.

Feel the silk scarves wrapped around your feet and calves. Let the soft fabric merge into your muscles and nerves, releasing any tension in your lower legs. Let this flow of soft silk flow up to your knees and into your thighs and hips until your hips and legs collapse into another soft pile of silk scarves.

Now your whole body is a pile of soft silk scarves, with one draped across your cheeks and another still there at your fingertips. You feel as loose and relaxed as piles of silk scarves, just lying there, soft and silky. Lie there and relax for as long as you wish, soft as silk, inside and out.

Practice this process as often as you like to relax and bring comfort to your body. If you prefer, you can substitute the silk scarf with the memory of a good massage, a warm Jacuzzi, or other positive experiences of normal sensory activity in your body.

NOTES

_____

_____

_____

_____

_____

_____

Tactful T

Table, Tabular, Tact, Tactful, Tactile, Take, Talent, Talisman, Talk, Tame, Tangible, Task, Taste, Tasteful, Tasty, Teach, Teachable, Teacher, Team, Technical, Technique, Technology, Telepathy, Telephone, Telephoto, Telescope, Television, Tell, Temperance, Temperate, Temple, Tenacious, Tend, Tender, Terrific, Testament, Testify, Testimonial, Testimony, Text, Texture, Thank, Thanks, Thankful, Thanksgiving, Theater, Theme, Theology, Theory, Therapeutic, Therapist, Therapy,

Thermostat, Thesis, Theurgy, Thick, Think, Thinker, Thorn, Thorough, Thought, Thoughtful, Thrifty, Thrive, Ticket, Tickle, Time, Timeless, Timely, Time-saving, Timing, Today, Toilet, Tolerant, Tomorrow, Tone, Tonic, Torch, Total, Touch, Touchstone, Town, Toy, Trade, Trademark, Tradition, Trampoline, Trance, Tranquil, Transcend, Transcendent, Transform, Transfusion, Transmigrate, Transmitter, Transmutation, Transparent, Transpire, Transplant, Transport, Transportation, Transvalue, Trapeze, Travel, Treasure, Treasury, Treat, Treatise, Treatment, Treaty, Tree, Tremendous, Tribe, Triumph, Triumphant, Troubadour, Truce, True, True-blue, True-love, Trust, Trustworthy, Trusty, Truth, Tune, Turning Point, Twinkle, Twinkling

ADD YOUR OWN GOLDEN T WORDS

_____

_____

_____

_____

_____

TABLE: A piece of furniture with vertical legs that support a flat surface where objects can rest and people can gather to talk, meet, and/or eat

TABULAR: Information or data organized in a table

TACT: Discretion, consideration

TACTFUL: The ability to say or do the considerate, kind thing in a delicate situation

TACTILE: Able to perceive through the sense of touch

TAKE: To accept into one's possession

TALENT: A natural or acquired aptitude for a physical or mental skill

TALISMAN: An object believed to confer protection or power

TALK: To speak or converse

TAME: Friendly, gentle

TANGIBLE: Able to be touched

TASK: Something that needs to be done

TASTE: Eating, drinking; experiencing

TASTEFUL: In good taste

TASTY: Delicious flavor

TEACH: Share knowledge through instruction

TEACHABLE: Able to be taught

TEACHER: A person who teaches

TEAM: An organized group of people working together

TECHNICAL: Specialized technique

TECHNIQUE: A systematic method or system for accomplishing a task

TECHNOLOGY: A practical application of technical knowledge

TELEPATHY: Engaging in conversation without words

TELEPHONE: Electronic communication using a handset

TELEPHOTO: A lens for seeing, enlarging, and taking photos of distant or near objects with blurred backgrounds

TELESCOPE: An instrument for looking at distant objects

TELEVISION: A device for receiving audio and video

TELL: To narrate a story or other communication

TEMPERANCE: The practice of self-control

TEMPERATE: Moderate, mild

TEMPLE: A place used for worship

TENACIOUS: Persistent

TEND: To cultivate or take care of

TENDER: Delicate, vulnerable; gentle

TERRIFIC: Astounding

Testament: A document providing directions for disbursing property after one's death

Testify: To serve as a witness under oath

Testimonial: A written or verbal recommendation testifying to a fact

Testimony: Evidence to support facts

Text: The words of something written

Texture: The way something feels to the touch

Thank, Thanks: An expression of gratitude

Thankful: Grateful, appreciative

Thanksgiving: A prayer or blessings to give thanks

Theater: The performance of a story on stage

Theme: A topic for discussion

Theology: An organized, rational study of the nature of God

Theory: A hypothesis based on organized knowledge

Therapeutic: Healing, curative

Therapist: One who conducts therapy

Therapy: A therapeutic treatment meant to heal illness or injury

Thermostat: A device that triggers temperature regulation

Thesis: A proposition

Theurgy: Divine intervention

Thick: Deep

Think: To reason or consider

Thinker: A reflective person

Thorn: A sharp barb that protects the rose

Thorough: Done fully, finished

Thought: The act of thinking

Thoughtful: Considerate, meditative

Thrifty: Capable in money management and the use of other resources

Thrive: Prosper, flourish

Ticket: A receipt showing payment for an event or service; what is needed

Tickle: To fill with pleasure

Time: An interval during which events occur from past to present

Timeless: Everlasting, unchanging

Timely: Well-timed

Time-saving: Efficient

Timing: Good judgment in when to act in order to achieve one's goal

Today: The present time

Toilet: Grooming, bathing

Tolerant: Open-minded

Tomorrow: The day after today

Tone: A sound or color

Tonic: Something that is medicinal or restorative

Torch: A tool for illumination

Total: The entirety

Touch: To affect emotionally; to come into contact

Touchstone: A standard

Town: A settlement

Toy: An object for amusement or play

Trade: A craft; an exchange of one item for another

Trademark: A symbol that identifies a product or device that's restricted to use by the owner/manufacturer

Tradition: Customs passed from one generation to another

Trampoline: Stretched fabric on a frame used for jumping

Trance: A hypnotic state

Tranquil: Serene, steady

Transcend: To exceed, rise above

Transcendent: Going beyond the limitations of ordinary experience

Transform: Renovate; change shape; undergo change

Transfusion: To inject blood or plasma into someone's bloodstream for healing

Transmigrate: Move from one body or place to another

TRANSMITTER: A device for broadcasting communications

TRANSMUTATION: The transformation of one element into another, such as base metals into gold

TRANSPARENT: Clear, easily understood

TRANSPIRE: Come to light

TRANSPLANT: To relocate as in a plant, a residence, or a body organ

TRANSPORT: To carry something from one place to another

TRANSPORTATION: The means for transporting something such as a train, truck, or plane

TRANSVALUE: To evaluate something by a standard that varies from the norm

TRAPEZE: A suspended bar or swing for acrobatics

TRAVEL: To journey from one place to another

TREASURE: Valuables

TREASURY: A place to store valuables

TREAT: Pleasure, delight, delicacy

TREATISE: A systematic, written account on a subject

TREATMENT: The use of remedies for healing

TREATY: A formal agreement between two or more countries

TREE: A large plant with a trunk, branches, and leaves

TREMENDOUS: Marvelous

TRIBE: A group sharing common interests or ancestry

TRIUMPH: A win, victory, or success

TRIUMPHANT: To feel pride in victory

TROUBADOUR: Love poet

TRUCE: A peace

TRUE: Genuine, real

TRUE-BLUE: Loyal

TRUE-LOVE: One's sweetheart

TRUST: Confidence in the integrity of a person

TRUSTWORTHY: Reliable

TRUSTY: Dependable

TRUTH: Honesty

TUNE: A melody

TURNING POINT: Crossroads; critical moment of change

TWINKLE: Sparkly

TWINKLING: An instant

WRITE YOUR FAVORITE GOLDEN T WORDS HERE

_____

_____

_____

_____

_____

NOW USE YOUR FAVORITE GOLDEN T WORDS
TO CREATE YOUR OWN MANTRA OR AFFIRMATION

_____

_____

_____

_____

_____

Tool: Tunnel of Trust

The phrase "light at the end of the tunnel" inspires trust during scary, challenging, unfamiliar times that have an unknown ending. At those times, you stand in the dark, sometimes paralyzed, wondering when the tunnel will open up to that light—but the tunnel is dark for a reason. Darkness renders the senses useless. You can't sense anything in the usual way so you're forced to use your intuitive tools to navigate: your inner eye, your inner voice, your body signals, and environmental cues. When you use your intuitive tools, their answers light your way.

As I worked through the transition from full-time work in education to starting my own private practice, the tunnel felt very dark at times. I had to make this change for health reasons, and what I planned fit nicely with my interests and dreams, but some people were concerned about my future, which increased my anxiety. I wanted their support, but I also had to figure out the best choice for myself. As a teacher, my earnings were high, I had a great position, and I would have had a better pension in a few more years. I had my own concerns about giving up that security, but I had no other choice. At that moment of knowing I had to do what was best for my health, what needed to be done became so clear it radiated a light of its own to guide my way. As I continued on my path, the more I stayed with the goals that felt right to me, the more everything fell into place. The path began to unfold before me so I could get to where I was going—the light at the end of the tunnel. Only once I opened up to my intuition, the tunnel's geography changed. It wasn't a dark tunnel anymore because I was no longer lost. The tunnel was dark only when I questioned myself. As soon as I trusted my own decisions, the light appeared.

To connect to your own intuitive tools to light your way through the dark tunnel, find a comfortable place to sit down. Take a few deep breaths in through your nose and out through your nose or mouth. Then let your breathing become natural as you relax into this process.

Find yourself in your own dark tunnel. How do you feel? Anxious? Excited? Angry? Giddy? Do you have mixed feelings or is one feeling predominant? Are the feelings based on resistance and blocks in your way as you move through the tunnel? Are there people or self-concepts in your path? Stand up to them, ask them to move aside, and step forward. Watch them melt away into the dark sides of the tunnel, opening up the way for you to move freely.

Are there other feelings holding you back? Are they feelings based on lack of knowledge or understanding of how to reach your goal? Ride those feelings to the questions you have about what you're doing. If you need answers to these questions, write them down so you can seek assistance.

Do you need encouragement or other support to move through your tunnel? Can you call on an internal resource or reach out to someone for support? Whose faces or names pop up to help you? Let those people emerge from the dark walls of the tunnel to walk with you.

Allow the light of your own clarity to lead the way. What is your next step as you move forward? Get support? Seek knowledge and information? Something else? If you're not sure, ask yourself, "What's next?" Allow the answer to present itself in the predominant mode you use to gather intuitive information: pictures, words, symbols, sounds, smells, and feelings.

Take notes on this information, which is the beginning of your map showing you the way through the tunnel. A feeling of relief and sense of trust accompanies this information because it's not at the level of the mind, which goes round and round in self-questioning and doubt. Instead, this map will shed light on your tunnel with a feeling of certainty and trust.

Repeat this exercise as needed to stay in touch with the map of your dark tunnel. Watch for signs as the dark tunnel gives way to the feeling that you're in the right place at the right time.

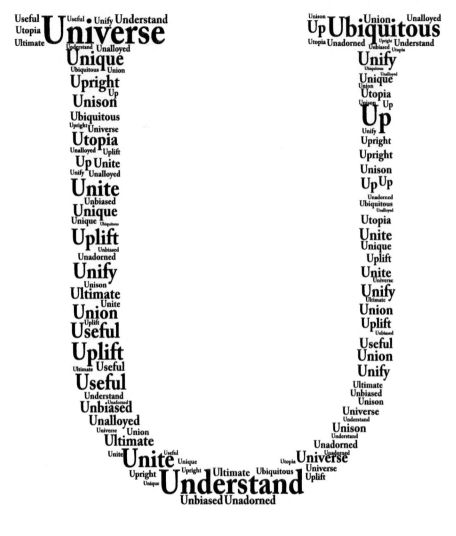

Uplifting U

Ubiquitous, Ultimate, Unadorned, Unalloyed, Unbiased, Understand, Unify, Union, Unique, Unison, Unite, Unity, Universal, Universe, Up, Upgrade, Uplift, Uplifting, Upright, Useful, Utopia

ADD YOUR OWN GOLDEN U WORDS

UBIQUITOUS: Seeming to be in all places at once

ULTIMATE: Fundamental; the greatest

UNADORNED: Genuine

UNALLOYED: Pure

UNBIASED: Impartial

UNDERSTAND: To comprehend the importance of something

UNIFY: To join together into a whole

UNION: Alliance

UNIQUE: One of a kind

UNISON: In harmony, agreement

UNITE: To make whole

UNITY: A harmonious whole

UNIVERSAL: Affecting the world

UNIVERSE: Everything in existence

UP: Positive

UPGRADE: A progressive improvement

UPLIFT: To raise to an improved spiritual, emotional, mental, or physical state

UPLIFTING: Inspiring, strengthening, elevating

UPRIGHT: Respectable

Useful: Beneficial

Utopia: A place of perfection

WRITE YOUR FAVORITE GOLDEN U WORDS HERE

_____

_____

_____

_____

_____

NOW USE YOUR FAVORITE GOLDEN U WORDS TO CREATE YOUR OWN MANTRA OR AFFIRMATION

_____

_____

_____

_____

_____

Tool: Universal You

Throughout time, spiritual leaders have brought the message that we're all the same, just packaged differently. Despite our connection to one another and all of mankind, it's easy to get caught up in our own lives and feel that the world—our world—is small and temporary. But we're all connected and remembering that can bring a much-needed perspective to a difficult moment.

I've used this guided meditation many times with elementary school children to remind them that their lives are bigger than a schoolroom, where popularity contests and peer-pressured behaviors can thrive. Outside the four walls, countless experiences are available for enriching their prospects and nourishing their dreams.

The children who've done this activity share a direct experience of their own expansive and universal nature. It's good to know who you are when you're young and remember that as you grow into an adult because the world outside of school also has some of the same drama that happens in schools. But knowing that you're universal empowers you to make a difference—and realize that your reach is far and wide. You are universal *and* significant—regardless of any drama that may occur.

Find a place to sit and relax. Take a few deep breaths in through your nose and out through your nose or mouth. Relax deeply into your chair and let your breathing become natural. Follow your breath to the center of your heart. Imagine a golden flame there whose light is pure joy. This is the kind of joy that dances spontaneously and wakes up with a smile.

Let the light of your joy expand from the center of your heart to fill your whole body. Feel your joy flow down into your fingertips and toes.

Allow the light of joy to expand beyond your body to the people sitting near you, then to your neighbors, and all the people in your town.

Imagine your joy expanding to the entire state you live in. Then let your joy flow to your whole country. Watch as your joy flows around the entire Earth wrapping the planet in a blanket of happiness. Allow your ever-expanding joy to radiate outward to the entire universe, touching all of space, all the stars and planets, and going beyond to infinity.

Now that your joy has grown so large, choose someone to focus on with whom you'd like to share your joy: a family member or friend; a person who challenges you; people in developing countries who are suffering from hunger, disease, or the ravages of civil war; people who work hard to take care of their families; people who are lonely for friendship; or even people who are already joyful. Let your joy be like a shower washing over them.

Now slowly bring your large awareness back from the universe to the planet, your country, your state, your town, your neighborhood, and now to the place where you're sitting and back to the center of your heart.

The universe of joy in your own heart has just touched the far reaches of the planet and the corners of the universe. You have no idea how your intention and experience of expanding your joy has touched others, but in your own expansive joy, you've uplifted yourself, connected to your planetary community, and practiced experiencing a part of yourself that will now permeate your day and touch all those you meet. Welcome, Universal You.

NOTES

_____

_____

_____

_____

_____

_____

_____

Visionary V

Vacation, Valedictorian, Valentine, Valiant, Valid, Validate, Valor, Valuable, Value, Variety, Vast, Vegetable, Velvet, Venerable, Veracious, Verb, Verbal, Verdant, Verify, Verily, Veritable, Vernal, Versatile, Verse, Viable, Vibrant, Victory, Vigor, Vigorous, Vim, Virile, Virtue, Virtuous, Vishuddha, Visible, Vision, Visionary, Visit, Vista, Visualize, Vital, Vitality, Vitalize, Vitals, Viva, Vivacious, Vivid,

Vocabulary, Vocal, Vocation, Voice, Volant, Voluntary, Vote, Vouch, Vow, Voyage, Voyageur, Vulnerable

ADD YOUR OWN GOLDEN V WORDS

_____

_____

_____

_____

_____

VACATION: A time for rest, pleasure, and relaxation,
 away from the obligations of work

VALEDICTORIAN: The highest academic standing
 for a student

VALENTINE: A person considered to be one's sweetheart,
 especially on Valentine's Day

VALIANT: Courageous, brave

VALID: Able to be supported with evidence

VALIDATE: Confirm

VALOR: Courage in battle

VALUABLE: Precious, useful

VALUE: The worth, merit or significance of something or someone

VARIETY: An assortment, diversity

VAST: Of great quantity or size, enormous

VEGETABLE: An edible part of a plant;
 a source of nourishment

Velvet: Smooth, soft fabric with a thick pile

Venerable: Worthy of respect

Veracious: Honest, truthful

Verb: A word that expresses action and existence

Verbal: Concerned with spoken or written words

Verdant: Lush green growth

Verify: Substantiate the truth with evidence

Verily: Confidently

Veritable: Unquestionable

Vernal: During the springtime

Versatile: Having varied abilities
    or functions

Verse: A line of poetry

Viable: Able to be sustained

Vibrant: Filled with energy, life

Victory: Success, triumph

Vigor: Lively

Vigorous: Robust

Vim: Exuberant vitality

Virile: Masculine strength

Virtue: Moral integrity

Virtuous: Upright, honorable

Vishuddha: The throat chakra, which corresponds
    to speech and self-expression

Visible: Able to be seen

Vision: Ability to see

Visionary: Capable of foresight

Visit: To go to see a place or a person

Vista: View onto a landscape

Visualize: To imagine something

Vital: Necessary; filled with life

VITALITY: The energy of life

VITALIZE: To fill with life energy

VITALS: Crucial physical organs

VIVA: A salute to life

VIVACIOUS: Spirited, lively

VIVID: Clear, brilliant

VOCABULARY: The words of a language

VOCAL: Having a voice

VOCATION: An occupation for which one is well suited

VOICE: The opportunity or right to express oneself

VOLANT: Being able to fly

VOLUNTARY: To act on free will

VOTE: One's preference in a formal election or the like

VOUCH: To verify, guarantee

VOW: A pledge or promise

VOYAGE: A long journey of discovery

VOYAGEUR: A guide on a voyage

VULNERABLE: Open to harm (e.g., as a newborn, child, elderly person, or someone who takes risks)

WRITE YOUR FAVORITE GOLDEN V WORDS HERE

_____

_____

_____

_____

_____

NOW USE YOUR FAVORITE GOLDEN V WORDS
TO CREATE YOUR OWN MANTRA OR AFFIRMATION

_____

_____

_____

_____

_____

Tool: Recover Your Voice

I've worked with several people who wanted to find their voice, including those with intuitive, verbal, and vocal gifts they used in their respective fields. You might never have guessed that these individuals felt the need to find their voice. Even when people have cultivated their gifts and made headway in their careers, it doesn't mean they've fully embodied their own voice.

In many countries, citizens enjoy freedom of speech as their right. Even so, when going to public school we're taught to talk at the proper time, wait our turn, save our ideas for another time, and almost always focus on topics we don't choose ourselves. I believe schools should teach important social skills and content knowledge, but in large classes of students, some students invariably get more airtime than others. This happens in families, too. The result may be learning to swallow your voice time and again to be in sync with the rules and dynamics of the prevailing system.

A few signs of a misplaced voice include increased anxiety speaking to others, devaluing your self-expression, and a constant lump in your throat. With my clients, I can often see when their voice gets stuck, because they swallow hard, as if they're pushing down their self-expression. The hard swallow might even represent an emotion or an expression of inspiration and joy.

To get in touch with the lost parts of your voice, find a comfortable place to sit and focus on your throat chakra. Your throat chakra is the fifth chakra, located at the physical throat, and its color is blue. An open throat chakra represents the ability to speak your truth, which lies beyond cultural, social, and familial conditioning. Your throat chakra also represents your creative self-expression. When you doubt and hold back your own truth and inner wisdom, your throat chakra closes down. Being able to make boundaries that allow you to live your truth also supports the opening of your throat chakra.

Breathe slowly and naturally. When it comes time to swallow, notice any place in your throat where your swallow feels hard with tension. Follow the swallow into the center of the tension. See if the tension has a shape or color for you. Then move through the tension up into your soft palate and toward the back of your throat. Follow this energy up to your third eye, which is located between your eyebrows (see more about the third eye chakra in "Ten Steps to Relaxation and Self-Hypnosis") and allow any images, sounds, and feelings to arise that give you insight about the tension.

You may be surprised by what bubbles up, so be patient and let it happen. As feelings arise or information comes, speak aloud. Speaking aloud is an important part of recovering your voice. If you weren't allowed to be angry and something that angers you comes up, sit there and speak the anger. Please note, I'm not advocating you go and get angry at someone. I'm suggesting you can accept and express the feeling aloud to yourself. Always cool off before deciding what to do when you feel a strong emotion. Consult with a trained individual for advice if you have difficulty resolving emotions that come up.

As emotions clear, notice what happens. Does the tension soften or change in some way? If it had a shape or color, how did that change? Do you feel clearer after speaking your voice? In what way does speaking your voice move you to live your truth or express yourself creatively? Allow your inspiration to rise up. Perhaps you have an urge to laugh or a creative idea comes to you. Let your ideas flow and take notes. Finally, no matter what comes up, decide how you'll proceed to express your unique voice in ways that are beneficial to you and others.

NOTES

_____

_____

_____

_____

_____

_____

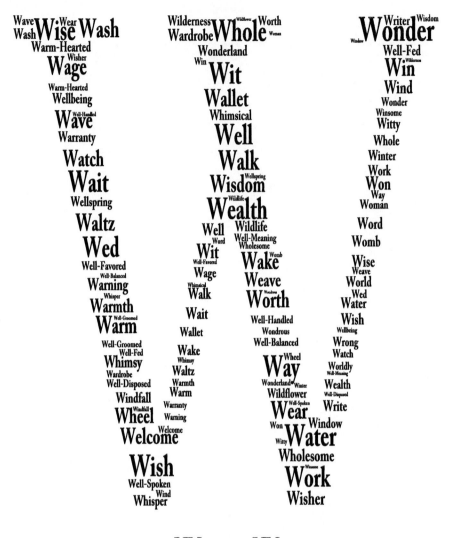

Warm W

Wage, Wait, Wake, Walk, Wallet, Waltz, Wardrobe, Warm, Warmth, Warning, Warranty, Wash, Watch, Water, Wave, Way, We, Wealth, Wear, Weave, Wed, Welcome, Well, Well-balanced, Well-being, Well-disposed, Well-favored, Well-fed, Well-groomed, Well-handled, Well-meaning, Well-spoken, Wellspring, Well-wisher, Wheel, Whimsical, Whimsy, Whisper, Whole, Wholehearted, Wholesome, Wilderness, Wildflower, Wildlife, Willing, Win,

Wind, Windfall, Window, Winner, Winsome, Winter, Wisdom,
Wise, Wish, Wit, Witness, Witty, Woman, Womb, Won, Wonder,
Wonderful, Wonderland, Wonderment, Wondrous, Word, Work,
World, Worldly-wise, Worth, Write, Writer, Wrong

ADD YOUR OWN GOLDEN **W** WORDS

_____

_____

_____

_____

_____

WAGE: Payment in exchange for services

WAIT: To pause for someone to catch up;
     to stay in anticipation of an event

WAKE: To stir into awareness

WALK: To move on foot one step after another

WALLET: A case where people keep money

WALTZ: A task that's easily attained

WARDROBE: A place to keep clothes; clothes

WARM: Heartfelt

WARMTH: Friendliness

WARNING: Information in advance of danger

WARRANTY: Assurance of quality

WASH: Cleanse

WATCH: Observe

WATER: Clear liquid essential for life on Earth

WAVE: A ripple in the ocean; a movement of the hand in greeting or farewell

WAY: A route from one location to another; a method

WE: A pronoun used to represent two or more people

WEALTH: Riches, abundance

WEAR: To put clothing on the body

WEAVE: A construction of interlacing threads

WED: To join; marry

WELCOME: Invited in with pleasure

WELL: Healthy

WELL-BALANCED: Sensible, regulated

WELL-BEING: State of happiness and health

WELL-DISPOSED: Likely to be sympathetic and kind

WELL-FAVORED: Attractive

WELL-FED: Having enough to eat, nourished

WELL-GROOMED: Attention to neatness and cleanliness in appearance

WELL-HANDLED: Well-managed

WELL-MEANING: Having good intentions

WELL-SPOKEN: Articulate; considerate in speech

WELLSPRING: A source of plenty

WELL-WISHER: Someone who wants good fortune for another

WHEEL: A circular object that rotates

WHIMSICAL: Playful

WHIMSY: Fancy

WHISPER: Quiet speech

WHOLE: Sound; complete

WHOLEHEARTED: Done with all one's heart and sincerity

WHOLESOME: Healthy, sensible

WILDERNESS: An uncultivated, natural region of nature

WILDFLOWER: A flower growing in the wild

WILDLIFE: Animals and plants that live in nature

WILLING: Ready to do something

WIN: Success, victory

WIND: Moving air

WINDFALL: Sudden good fortune

WINDOW: An opening in a building that lets in light

WINNER: One who wins

WINSOME: Charming

WINTER: The coldest season of the year,
when it often snows in colder climates

WISDOM: Good judgment, common sense, learned

WISE: Sensible, prudent

WISH: A desire for something

WIT: Intelligence, resourcefulness

WITNESS: Someone who hears or sees something

WITTY: Humorous, clever

WOMAN: A female human

WOMB: The place in a female mammal where new life grows;
a protected place

WON: Achieved; acquired

WONDER: Admiration, astonishment

WONDERFUL: Excellent

WONDERLAND: An amazing imaginary place

WONDERMENT: Awe

WONDROUS: Remarkable

WORD: A combination of sounds put together to
symbolize meaning

Work: A means for earning a living

World: The planet Earth; the universe

Worldly-wise: Experienced in human affairs

Worth: Valuable

Write: To put words and sentences on paper
to create a composition

Writer: One who writes, an author

Wrong: An error

WRITE YOUR FAVORITE GOLDEN **W** WORDS HERE

_____

_____

_____

_____

_____

NOW USE YOUR FAVORITE GOLDEN **W** WORDS
TO CREATE YOUR OWN MANTRA OR AFFIRMATION

_____

_____

_____

_____

_____

Tool: Spirit Walkers

Like a dragonfly larva that begins its life in a muddy pond, many of us swim our way through a murky life, fighting off predators, searching for food and a mate, and aiming to build a life of love, security, fun, and significance. But dragonfly larvae don't slink around in the mud forever. They shed their skin several times, then crawl out of the pond, lock onto a branch, and emerge as new beings. Each larva becomes a glorious creature of brilliant blue, vivid red, emerald green, bright orange, or other shades of the rainbow, with lacy wings that reflect sunlight, enticing children and nature lovers to chase them around ponds, alongside streams, and through meadows of wildflowers.

Like the dragonfly, we're not just little larvae crawling around in the muck. We can crawl out and give our wings a chance to glitter in the sun. We're spirit walkers—embodied spirits walking around on the Earth temporarily in our physical bodies.

Find a comfortable place to sit and relax. Close your eyes and think about the material world. It feels solid yet, from studying the atomic composition of the universe, we know it's mostly empty space. The particles that make up a solid object interact in such a way that objects only *appear* solid.

Observe your breath flowing in and out in a gentle rhythm. Allow your breath to slow down. Imagine your body, which feels quite solid, but is mainly water, empty space, and the energy of your life-giving spirit. Follow your breath in and observe how it permeates all your inner spaces. Then allow your breath to flow out and observe how it expands and flows into the external world.

Continue to follow your breath as it enters all the spaces within yourself and all the spaces of the external world. Travel deeper and deeper into those spaces until your sense of solidity gives way to the porous spaces of matter. Imagine the vibration of spirit flowing through all those spaces with its expansive nature. Allow the in-breath and the out-breath to come together as the boundaries of your physical body melt away in the vast collection of life energies connected by the breath. Continue practicing this breathing pattern for 5 to 15 minutes.

Variation: Choose a golden word to carry inside you on the inhalation, and breathe out on the exhalation. For example, breathe in "health" on the inhalation, and breathe out "health" on the exhalation. While voicing the word to yourself, imagine the power of the word bathing you in its meaning on each inhalation. On each exhalation, imagine the power of the word saturating your external life with its meaning. Take time to form images and feelings of what the word means to you.

If you feel your golden word more easily inside than outside, send the inside feeling to your outer environment. Observe how sending that feeling outward changes your experience and the possibilities for you. You can also practice the reverse. If you feel the golden word more clearly outside yourself, then breathe it in and observe how it changes you on the inside. Let your creative imagination go to work and design possibilities for you.

NOTES

_____

_____

_____

_____

_____

XO X

XO, X-ray, X-ray Therapy, Xenial, Xenodochial,
Xenophile, Xenophilia, X-factor

ADD YOUR OWN GOLDEN X WORDS

_____

_____

_____

_____

_____

XO: A kiss and a hug

X-ray: Photograph with X-rays

X-ray Therapy: Therapy with X-rays

Xenial: Hospitable

Xenodochial: Friendly to strangers

Xenophile: Someone who loves the unknown

Xenophilia: A love for the unknown

X-factor: A variable that could have a significant impact
on a situation

WRITE YOUR FAVORITE GOLDEN X WORDS HERE

_____

_____

_____

_____

_____

NOW USE YOUR FAVORITE GOLDEN **X** WORDS
TO CREATE YOUR OWN MANTRA OR AFFIRMATION

_____

_____

_____

_____

_____

Tool: The X-Factor (Listen to Inner Whispers)

You hear your inner voice talking to you, but you ignore it. We all do. We think we know better. You're driving in your car, and you have the urge to drive a different way home, but you pay no attention, thinking, "That other way is so much longer and really inconvenient. Forget it. I'm going the usual way." Then, you find yourself in a traffic jam, a gapers' block, or a blocked lane due to construction. You kick yourself for not listening. You knew, but didn't take advantage. What else have you missed by giving your inner voice the cold shoulder?

Three days before my dad's stroke, in February of 2007, I heard my inner voice urge me to stop at his office for a visit, but work was busy, so I didn't get there. Besides, our relationship was conflicted and I didn't want any grief. When I got the news of his stroke, I was gripped with regret. What might have been said in those last few minutes? What might have happened had I listened and opened myself up one more time? I'd let my fears impact me more than I'd trusted my inner voice. It's at times like this that listening to my inner voice seems crazy. Could it be wrong?

In my twenties, I was in advertising looking for a job. I had left a small graphic design studio that went bankrupt, had a good portfolio of copywriting and print production samples, but there just didn't seem to be any jobs. One rainy afternoon I fell into despair and began to pray. *Dear God, please help me find a job.* After 30 minutes of prayer and silence, I heard the words, "Go to Rizzoli." *Why?* I wondered. Rizzoli was a bookstore at Water Tower Place. Was I supposed to leave advertising and work for minimum wage in a downtown bookstore? But I had asked— and I'd actually received an answer.

So I put on a skirt and walked to Rizzoli under my umbrella in a light drizzle. Fifteen minutes later, I arrived at Water Tower Place, shook the rain off my umbrella, and pulled it closed. I took the escalator up to Rizzoli and, not knowing what the heck I was doing there, tried to prepare myself for the unexpected.

When I asked the clerk about a job, he replied, "Oh, we don't advertise in the store. You'll have to look in the *Reader* for job openings." I nodded and smiled. So this was why I had to go to Rizzoli—to get me to look at the *Reader?* I'd considered the *Reader* an alternative paper, not a serious place for job-hunting, so I hadn't looked there. I found a paper on my way home, then made myself comfortable on the sofa and paged through it. There it was: a tiny advertisement looking for someone who could manage print production and write copy. My mind stopped in its tracks at how this unexpected gift had fallen into my lap. The combination of skills was perfect for me at the time. I applied for, interviewed, and got the job— my first salaried job.

I call this kind of inner guidance the X-factor: a variable in a situation that has an unpredictable impact. Following our intuition may seem strange and illogical at first, but the results can be spectacular. If we could have accomplished the same outcome with a linear approach, we would have. Unfortunately, many of us wait to follow our intuition until our other options have run out.

The X-factor is about your personal experiment in listening to your intuition, even if it doesn't make sense at the time. Learning to separate that voice, feeling, or premonition from all the competing mental and environmental noise takes practice, but everyone has it, everyone's heard it, and everyone has both regrets from ignoring it and celebrations from following it. Just think back to those times when you followed it and you'll remember what it is you're looking for. Also, our intuition never asks us to put ourselves or others in harm's way.

NOTES

Youthful Y

Yang, Yay, Yearn, Yes, Yield, Yin, Yippee, Yoga, Yogi,
Yogini, Young, Youth, Youthful, Yummy

ADD YOUR OWN GOLDEN Y WORDS

_____

_____

_____

_____

_____

YANG: The masculine principle in Chinese philosophy; active

YAY: An expression of victory

YEARN: A strong longing

YES: Affirmation, consent

YIELD: The product of cultivation, harvest

YIN: The female principle in Chinese philosophy; receptive

YIPPEE: An exclamation of delight

YOGA: A system of discipline for body and mind whose aim is to experience consciousness

YOGI, YOGINI: One who practices yoga

YOUNG: An early stage in a person's life or the life of a project

YOUTH: A young person or someone who has the qualities of youth

YOUTHFUL: Active and energetic like a young person

YUMMY: Delicious

WRITE YOUR FAVORITE GOLDEN Y WORDS HERE

_____

_____

_____

_____

NOW USE YOUR FAVORITE GOLDEN Y WORDS TO CREATE YOUR OWN MANTRA OR AFFIRMATION

_____

_____

_____

_____

Tool: Exchange Junk Food Yearnings for Real Food Yummies

Do you crave junk foods? Even the most strong-willed people I know can be defeated by a single chocolate-chip cookie. Why? Because where there's one cookie, an army of cookies waits in the wings. As a kid, I dipped Oreos in milk, nibbled pinwheel cookies in a spiral to the center, and crunched on salty chips. Later on, I graduated to expensive junk: Pepperidge Farm Milanos and Pirouettes. Really, any cookie that would melt in my mouth had a short shelf life in my house. When health food stores introduced their own version of junk food, I focused on salty potato chips followed by health food rice crispy bars. But who was I kidding? Health food junk food is no better than processed junk food, especially if it replaces real food.

What's your craving? Melt in your mouth sweets? Chewy cookies? Crunchy, salty, fatty chips? Salt followed by sugar followed by fat followed by regret, self-pity, and shame? One craving feeds another in a chain that leads right back to the beginning. Giving in brings temporary relief, but not long-term satisfaction. How have you addressed your cravings: with a feast or famine approach, or with gentle, self re-education?

I've done multiple sessions with clients on releasing cravings. I'd like to share these helpful techniques with you, which you can do at home or with the support of a hypnotist.

Please note: When you release a craving, it takes a few days for your body to readjust itself. When you decide to give up sugar or chips, please realize you may feel worse for a couple of days before you feel better. It's like quitting smoking. First your body has to rebalance. The first three to four days are the most difficult. Then you have to change the actual physical habit of reaching for that particular food and putting it into your mouth—but, thank goodness, you don't have to give up food entirely!

1. Enjoy Your Craving—in Your Imagination

What? Enjoy the craving? Yes, but not by gobbling up the treats. Imagining you are indulging is a way to transition from the cravings and feelings associated with it to a feeling of equanimity and control. When we give ourselves permission to enjoy something taboo, the mind and emotions come to rest, but enjoying your craving is different than actually giving in. You're not going to eat the food you crave. It's just a trick.

Being besieged by a food craving then caving into it can happen very quickly. You can slow down the process by rehearsing how you're going to manage the craving when you're not actually having one.

Start by imagining the taste of the food you want to give up. Close your eyes and take the time to smell the food, taste the food, and swallow the food—*in your imagination*. Enjoy it fully and without shame.

As you enjoy it, keep in mind that it's a manufactured food the company created to give your taste buds and your body's physiology such intense pleasure that it's difficult to resist. Each time you buy their food, they make a profit. When the food has little to offer in terms of nourishment, that profit is at your expense. But don't judge yourself. It's not your fault that your body's physiology has been taken advantage of by the food industry.

You can imagine all the places on your body where this junk food will come to rest. When I gave up sugar, I imagined it turning into fat that glued itself to my hips and thighs, which is exactly what had happened. Enjoy the imaginary, free food to your heart's delight as you relax and determine what you'd like to do or eat instead.

After a while, you won't think about the junk food anymore. An ex-smoker stops thinking about cigarettes at some point. When you leave a bad relationship, at first you miss the person, but when you remind yourself of why you left, you move on. Enjoy the fun part of your relationship with junk food in your imagination, but remember why you're breaking up and move on.

2. Determine What You Really Want

When you have a craving, you want something, but it's not the junk food that's going to satisfy you either emotionally or nutritionally. So as you enjoy the experience of your favorite junk food in your fantasy, drill down beneath the craving to see what you're really yearning for. What would satisfy you? Satisfying a junk food craving is only satisfying for a moment, then pain follows.

What do you yearn for that would bring relief, health, and long-lasting pleasure? A glass of water? A long walk? A nap? A hug? A good laugh? A good cry? Some quiet time? A deep breath? A sweet carrot? An egg? A handful of nuts? An early dinner? Talking to a friend? Reconnecting to your Self through meditation? Take a moment to re-orient yourself to your deeper needs and desires, the ones underlying your craving, to connect to your true needs. Whatever it is, make a decision to take care of it. Make a list of ways you'd like to nourish your true, underlying needs.

_____

_____

_____

_____

_____

3. Move On

After you've fully enjoyed your food fantasy, drink two large glasses of water. Often when you have a craving or a hunger pang, you're just thirsty. If there's true hunger, you'll know in about 15 or 20 minutes.

When I talk to people about drinking more water, here's what I often hear: "But I'll have to, you know, go to the bathroom more." That's right. Drinking water hydrates your body, supports important physiological processes, and cleans you out. Most people want to detox, but they don't want to use the bathroom. I think you'll be pleased at how much better you feel just from drinking enough water. About half your weight in ounces, more if you have a high activity level, is the recommended daily amount of water.

If you have time, go for a short walk. Otherwise, get busy for about 15 minutes with a physical task to distract yourself such as doing a load of laundry, washing the dishes, cleaning your bird feeders, cleaning the bathroom, changing the sheets on your bed, or catching up on other chores. If you're at work, take a walk down the hall to run an errand or talk to someone. Interrupt your pattern with a physical activity.

4. Eat a Whole Foods Snack

If you're still hungry after two glasses of water, your walk, or other distraction, eat a healthy snack of your choice from the family of whole foods: fruits, vegetables, proteins, and fats. Considering you've just resisted eating an unhealthy, high-calorie food, eat whatever you want that's a whole food. A whole food is real food as opposed to processed food. Real food grows from a plant source or comes from an animal. Some examples are carrots, cucumbers, red peppers, peanut butter, cashews, apples, oranges, plain yogurt, a slice of meat or fish, a hard-boiled egg, a bowl of rice or oatmeal, and so on.

I've learned from experience that people have contradictory ideas about eating a whole food snack. "I'll get so full!" they say. "I really don't want to eat that much!" Whole food snacks, depending on what you choose, have fiber, fats, and proteins that naturally fill you up. They satisfy a true hunger, whereas junk foods don't. Because the junk food lacks "substance" it provides a taste sensation with little bulk to satisfy your appetite. Yet the lack of substance in junk foods is the culprit in weight gain. Not feeling satisfied, there's no end to the eating. Eating real foods that satisfy you, and drinking enough water to hydrate you, brings an end to the junk food cycle, nourishment to your body, and pride to your ego for maintaining self-control.

If possible, when you eat your whole food snack, sit down, cut your food into pieces, taste one bite at a time, and chew thoroughly. Use herbs or sea salt to make your snack savory. Enjoy this snack with the same amount of sensory attention and gusto that you gave your food fantasy.

At first, the taste of whole foods may not give you the same explosive satisfaction as processed junk food. In fact, nothing will ever taste like the chemically processed food that lures you into addictive behavior. But in three to four days your mood will even out, your taste buds will wake up, and you'll have more true physical energy. In fact, you might find out you need some rest and have been using junk food to string your energy along. Soon, with improved food habits and a more natural body rhythm that you pay attention to, you'll wonder how you ever became enslaved to junk food.

As with changing any habit, the support of a hypnotist, health coach, or good friend can get you through the tough times and direct you to recipes for making your own healthy snacks. Gaining control over how you feed your body in the face of massive media advertising, cultural and social pressures, and the ease of eating processed foods deserves a massive celebration. Think of a non-food way that suits your personality and lifestyle to celebrate your wins. Write down those ideas here and make a commitment to following through.

_____

_____

_____

_____

_____

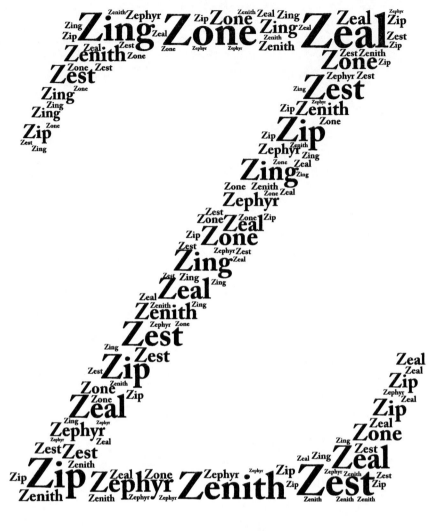

Zany Z

Zany, Zeal, Zenith, Zephyr, Zest, Zing, Zip, Zone

ADD YOUR OWN GOLDEN Z WORDS

_____

_____

_____

_____

_____

ZANY: Unconventional

ZEAL: Enthusiastic pursuit of a goal

ZENITH: The highest point, summit

ZEPHYR: A mild breeze

ZEST: Enthusiastic enjoyment

ZING: Lively

ZIP: Pep

ZONE: A state of flow

WRITE YOUR FAVORITE GOLDEN Z WORDS HERE

_____

_____

_____

_____

_____

NOW USE YOUR FAVORITE GOLDEN Z WORDS
TO CREATE YOUR OWN MANTRA OR AFFIRMATION

_____

_____

_____

_____

_____

Tool: Enter the Dream Zone

In the space between dreaming and sleeping, you can recall your dreams. Sometimes dreams have crazy, discombobulated images and textures that make little sense, but when you get in the habit of remembering and writing down your dreams, messages that have value in guiding your life come through. Despite the value of dreams, many people say, "I don't have time to lie there, remember my dreams, and then write them down. I barely have enough time for my life!"

If this sounds like you, consider taking just one day a week for this practice and see how it benefits you. I think you'll find the information you receive beneficial, insightful, and at times life-saving. The dream I shared in the preface is an example. If I hadn't been journaling my dreams, I would have missed the life-saving dream that kept me focused on a positive health outcome for nearly a decade. You'll also receive relationship, financial, and other information. Dreams are fun and entertaining, too, because the dream world can be like visiting Alice in Wonderland at times. So are your dreams worth remembering and writing down? There is no question as to the value of dreams to provide life-saving information. Your dreams are a treasure chest of information. Open it up and rummage around.

I got started with dream journaling after learning to meditate in 1985. I noticed that some of my nighttime dreams provided images that came true. I wanted to learn how to harness that information so I began keeping a dream journal. It took a while to learn how to remember my dreams, so I experimented.

Here's the technique I developed. First of all, to dream you'll need to get enough sleep. If you skimp on sleep, you won't spend enough time dreaming. Second, keep a journal by your bed because once you start moving around in the morning, remembering the subtle imagery and feelings from your dreams is interrupted by the pull of the material world and your to-do list. Then, finding your dreams again is like trying to catch the fog.

To remember your dreams, wake up slowly. Think of the space between waking and sleeping like a fogbank where you're floating and waiting in a receptive state for the fog to clear. If you're suddenly jarred awake, it's like blowing a foghorn. You'll be jarred out of dreamtime too soon and won't have access to the images, textures, and feelings floating around in the fog.

As you lie in a gentle sleep, on the threshold between worlds, barely awake, just wait there, resting. As soon as one part of a dream comes through, usually a trail of dreams follow. Don't think about them, just observe. Don't chase them; be receptive, like a magnet. Dreams are like the breeze. You can't chase the breeze. You have to wait for it to sweep over you.

When the dream sequence is complete, pick up your journal and jot down a few notes that will help you remember, especially if there was a seemingly unrelated sequence. Then write them down in as much detail as you can remember. Write on one page only and leave the facing page blank. As you write, notice how you feel and any other ideas you have about the dream's meaning. On the blank, facing page, write down those thoughts and feelings. When you're finished writing, go back to each dream and write additional ideas on the facing page about the dream that stand out to you.

At first, you may not understand the language of your dreams, but as you continue logging them in your journal, themes will emerge. For example, you may notice your dreams giving you information about something that's about to happen, either good or bad, but the symbols weren't clear except in retrospect. For example, there may be a clock that gives you a time, a calendar that gives you a date, a person's face who you plan to see in a few days, or something else that may represent the actual time or date of a future occurrence in your own or someone else's life. These symbols may be idiosyncratic to you so watch and learn what they are.

You may experience pain in a dream that foretells a difficult experience, or you may experience joys that predict good fortune. At times a dream will show you the physical context for a situation along with elements of the event. When you write down your dreams, you begin to notice how these elements fit together.

You may also notice how your thoughts and feelings from the day affect your dreams. Their presence can be comfortable or uncomfortable reminders of how our habitual thoughts creep into our dreams and further embed themselves in our lives. Noticing our mental patterns through dream journaling becomes an opportunity for celebrating or making changes in our habits of mind.

You can experiment with influencing your dreams by intentionally focusing on certain golden words, whose vibration you want to increase in your life, just before you go to sleep. You can also ask your dreams directly to help you with specific life challenges by focusing on them as you fall asleep.

As you become more adept at remembering your dreams and take time to write them down, I think you'll be grateful for the treasures you find. After 30 years of dream journaling, I don't always dream and sometimes my dreams drift away when I'm too busy to spend time in the dream zone. So don't give up if you don't succeed at this method right away or only have time to do this one or two days a week. With time and practice, your dreams will be as real to you as the information in the material world.

NOTES

_____

_____

_____

_____

_____

_____

_____

PART TWO

The

SCIENCE OF GOLDEN WORDS, MANTRAS, *and* HYPNOSIS

I

From Serene to Silly:
What Makes a Word *Golden*?

Better than a thousand words,
is one word that brings peace.

BUDDHA

In writing a book about golden words, I assure you I'm not making a case for excluding words from the English language. For better or for worse, we need all our words to express the range of human experience from calamity to miracle. Even though I've left out violent, disempowering, and unpleasant words, I don't deny the existence of those experiences.

The truth is, it's often *because* of our challenging experiences that we change for the better and seek ways to improve our own lives and the lives of others. In fact, no matter what may have happened to us, whether from our own free will or that of circumstances and people outside our control, an improved state of mind is always possible. *Life* happens, and flowers can grow in it when they're planted and cared for.

What's a Golden Word?

When I posed this question to clients and friends to get their points of view, I asked for their thoughts about positive words, since that's the term people use to talk about what I'm calling *golden* words. The main difference, I believe, is in the application. A word can be positive, but it becomes golden when used intentionally to create positive change. With this is in mind, I posed the following questions:

- What makes a word positive—to you?
- What do you think about emotion words?
- What are *your* positive words?

What their answers had in common were uplifting words like tenderness, harmony, joyful, blessed, loved, peaceful, free, and empowered. Everyone also agreed that emotions, though uncomfortable at times, are important parts of being human because they're necessary to experience in order to move toward a more positive perspective.

Some word preferences are subjective, based on personal experiences. For instance, people who love ice cream might consider the word "ice cream" to be positive, while those who are lactose-intolerant or struggle with food cravings have negative associations with the same phrase. Unlike actual ice cream, true golden words, like the ones in Part One of this book, have a universality that is not so easily undermined by individual subjectivities.

The contrast between uplifting words and uncomfortable emotions creates tension. Getting to the joy may require feeling vulnerable, walking through sadness, cultivating a healthy way to release frustration, hiking in the woods, eating healthy foods, going for a run, or learning emotional patience through meditation, mindfulness, or self-hypnosis. Addressing fear may require figuring out how to take a calculated risk. Experiencing the wonder of a rainbow may mean suspending cynicism and remembering a time of innocence. Moving into a positive place of hope could mean experiencing memories that feel uncomfortable and taking a step forward in trust. That's what it means to be human. Being positive isn't about fencing out human experiences, but rather embracing all that's human about our life and figuring out how to navigate it.

With this in mind, I developed 10 categories for choosing golden words using resources I'd gathered during 25 years in varied roles as educator, educational and health coach, hypnotist, children's yoga teacher, meditator, friend, daughter, sister, and partner. My sources, which include materials from education, hypnosis, coaching, meditation, psychology, and neuroscience, provide information you can use to shift into positive states.

Ten Kinds of Golden Words

In the rest of this chapter, I've identified and discussed 10 types of golden words. I've provided examples to show how these types of words can guide us to increasingly positive states. The words I've included in The Interactive Dictionary Toolkit were chosen based on these categories. If at first glance you don't agree that a word I've included is golden, I invite you to dig deeper into the meaning of that word and your personal association with it. You may just find a bridge to a positive state of mind, either through reflection or by using one of the tools I've provided with each letter of the alphabet.

TEN KINDS OF GOLDEN WORDS

1. Human emotion words
2. Happiness and acceptance words
3. Taking control and mastery words
4. Physical health words
5. Social words
6. Life purpose words
7. Uplifting words
8. Ways of knowing words

9. Metaphors, imagery, stories, and play words

10. Laughter words

1. Human Emotion Words

How many core emotions do humans have? In the 1980s, Paul Ekman's cross-cultural research on facial expressions identified six universal emotions: sadness, anger, fear, happiness, surprise, and disgust.[1] Later on, he added a seventh: contempt.[2] His final human emotions map was the result of considering 250 research studies.[3]

At the University of Glasgow, scientists who study emotions using technology to read dynamic facial expressions believe we have four basic categories of emotion including: fear/surprise (possibly from approaching danger), anger/disgust (possibly from stationary danger), happiness, and sadness.[4] The lead author of the study, Rachael Jack, says that fear and surprise share an initial facial expression, but subtle changes in the development of the facial expression enable us to tell the difference. Anger and disgust also share the same initial expression but develop differently. The slight differences between the shared expressions of fear/surprise and anger/disgust may indicate different types of danger.[5] Our other emotions are thought to be spinoffs from these four categories, possibly developed in social or cultural situations. The Glasgow team's five-minute YouTube presentation shows how they used technology to read dynamic facial expressions and gives a summary of their research.[6]

We sometimes feel multiple emotions at once, something that can be described as having *mixed feelings*, but we can think about them separately. Fear calls for an immediate response such as fight, flight, or freeze. Anger occurs when our boundaries have been crossed, and we have to stand up for ourselves. Sadness signals a loss, which you grieve before moving on to replace what's gone or to learn to live without it. Happiness lets you know that everything is okay—you're safe and sound.

These core emotional responses act as stoplights, providing important signals that tell us what actions we should take for our survival and well-being. A pitfall many of us face is getting mired in these emotions: stewing in our anger, for example, or expecting to be *only* happy. At other times we judge our emotions because they're uncomfortable or we think we *should* be positive. The irony is that these signals *are* positive. We don't want to be afraid, yet reflecting on fear signals helps us understand what's required to feel safe. Anxiety, a form of fear, can help us stop to consider the options and possibilities for action. Not allowing sadness to flow may prevent us from understanding what's needed to move on and reconnect.

SADNESS

Crying has many purposes. During my recovery, I read several books by Larry Dossey, a physician who writes about the spiritual dimensions of healing. In his book, *The Extraordinary Healing Power of Ordinary Things*, Dossey discusses the various types of tears. Tears may be a cry for help, such as when an infant cries or a person who's been injured physically or emotionally cries to attract help. In a Japanese study, patients with rheumatoid arthritis who cried in response to an emotional stimulus had better immune responses and improved more over the following year. Dossey suggests this finding may support the notion that crying relieves pain and inflammation so we ought to let it out instead of soldiering on. Finally, emotional tears were analyzed and found to contain more toxins than irritant tears (e.g., those from cutting onions), implying tears carry waste from the body.[7]

In the initial years of recovery from the physical trauma of my bike accident, I cried a lot. I lost my dad in many stages after his stroke, then he passed away. The physical pain I experienced made speaking and communicating so uncomfortable I had to limit my social life. I also experienced a life review of many memories, both happy and traumatic.

Crying helped me gain insight on those memories, find solutions to medical dilemmas, and synthesize my experiences into a more meaningful whole. With meaning and insight came peace.

Do you save up your tears and put on a good face? Letting go of grief that's been keeping a relationship, self-image, pain, or core beliefs fixed in place frees you to move into present time and make new, more empowering choices. Tears can be a positive chapter in the healing process, with a positive purpose.

ANGER

Anger can signal our boundaries have been crossed and it's time to say "no." Gabor Maté wrote an entire book about this called *When the Body Says No.* It turns out people with disabling, fatal illnesses often don't know when to say no. When I was working full time and involved in hours of weekly self-care, I had to learn to say no. It was a matter of survival. As I began to improve, this meant prioritizing so I could keep my obligations, but also have some fun. You've got to have some fun and joy in your life to heal. One way I freed up my schedule was by doing laundry less often. One day I told a friend it had been a month since I'd last done my laundry.

"A month?!" she exclaimed, obviously shocked by my apparent lack of hygiene.

"I don't have time," I replied, a bit defensive.

"But you have time to write and take pictures," she countered.

"Yes, because if I don't write and take pictures, I feel angry. And I don't want to be angry," I explained. "Dirty laundry doesn't make me angry," I laughed.

As I got better at balancing work, play, and relationships, I celebrated by doing a few loads of laundry.

Properly expressed, anger may have other health benefits. Candace Pert, the renowned pharmacologist who discovered the opiate receptor, says that outbursts of anger have been associated with spontaneous cancer recoveries—suggesting that anger can jumpstart the immune system.[8] You can take heart in the words of the Dalai Lama, too. In a *Time* magazine interview, the Dalai Lama was asked the question: *Do you ever feel angry or outraged?*

To which he answered, "Oh, yes, of course. I'm a human being. Generally speaking, if a human being never shows anger, then I think something's wrong. He's not right in the brain. [Laughs.]"[9]

FEAR

In a 2010 interview, neuroscientist Joseph LeDoux talked about the role of fear in human evolution: "All animals have to be able to detect danger and respond to danger in order to stay alive, including humans." The emotional processing hub in our brains forms associations between outside stimuli and "stamps in those experiences" regardless of whether they feel good or distressing. In fact, we need a fear response stamped into our brain so we can learn to avoid danger.[10]

Fortunately, we can soften stamped-in emotional responses through what LeDoux calls memory "reconsolidation." In reconsolidation, an emotional memory that's being retrieved, such as a trauma, becomes unstable. In this unstable state, new information can be incorporated, which changes the memory.[11] Just destabilizing the emotional part of the memory, then introducing new information, reduces the level of emotional discomfort in the traumatic memory. For this reason, allowing yourself to feel your emotions provides the opportunity to introduce information, shift your emotional state, and dial down the intensity of your emotional load. Reconsolidation can happen during hypnosis, coaching, therapy, self-reflection, talking to friends, getting bodywork, doing yoga, taking a walk, and countless other activities where we feel safe enough for the memory to emerge, talk about, and add a new perspective. Feeling our emotions is a powerful opportunity for change.

I had to address a paralyzing fear of riding my bike again. But after my dad passed away, I was determined. It was the fourth summer after my accident and I still experienced minor pain, but my mood was good so I decided it was time to ride through the woods and feel the wind on my face again.

I drove to my mom's house, where the bike was parked in her garage. My heart pounded just looking at it, but I stayed, determined to overcome my fear. I took the bike and walked it for a couple miles. Tears streamed down my face as I realized how dramatically that one ride had changed my life. I had a right to be scared, but as I walked, grief and fear turned to determination. My life may have changed radically because of one bike ride, but I had received many blessings from the accident, too. Getting back on would be another landmark and shift fear into courage. But being courageous didn't mean just jumping back on the bike. I had to think through how to approach this goal.

I looked at the statistics of bike accident concussions and learned that riding a bike is actually a dangerous sport. More deaths occur from cycling than any other recreational sport including football, snow skiing, and skateboarding.[12] Was it worth riding again? As I imagined myself gliding happily through the woods on a bike path I decided yes, it was, but created guidelines. I would ride in places designated for bikes and buy a new bike so I could sit upright. My fears subsided with these conscious decisions. I rode my new bike, an upright Electra Townie in bright blue, later that summer. Saddlebags and a *Wizard of Oz* front basket carried my photography equipment. I brought my bike to a nearby trail and triumphantly rode around the circle a few times.

In another example, I had a client who was facing the possibility of a life-threatening medical diagnosis. She had a right to be anxious. We talked through the questions she wanted to ask her doctor as well as possible options for managing her college courses. Then I offered her a hypnosis process where she could enter the treasure room of her subconscious to find resources that would support her during her upcoming medical tests. What she found there was her doctor and the word, "OK." She didn't know what the outcome would be, but she had the feeling from that experience that everything was okay. What she learned from her medical tests was that everything *was* okay. She left the doctor's office with a clean bill of health and moved on with her life. Our subconscious can provide valuable information that gives us consolation and support.

It takes time and energy to maintain our fears, time that could be spent finding resolution. But resolution doesn't mean diving in headfirst just to relieve the emotional tension or remaining paralyzed in fear. Rather, overcoming fear is about developing resources that support the search for what feels right, comfortable, safe, and balanced. This approach anchors your actions in thoughtfulness, which prepares you to face your fear from a place of self-care and emotional stability.

EMOTIONAL FLOW

Our emotional states continually flow and change, depending on what happens and needs to be done at the moment. These changing states are normal, human, and positive. It's what we do about them that can have repercussions, both positive and negative.

Fear can paralyze you unless you face it. Positive feelings, like love, may inspire you to call your partner, a parent, or friend to talk and make a positive connection. When you feel angry about the way you're treated and react without thinking, negative aftershocks can go on for sometime. Every emotion should not necessarily be acted on, but if we fight off our emotions and judge them, we miss an opportunity to be informed of their message. Then we get caught at an emotional intersection in a traffic jam.

When the Dalai Lama talks about anger as a natural, human emotion, or Joseph LeDoux talks about fear as a guide to survival, they're not advocating an irresponsible approach to self-expression. When I learned to meditate, I was taught to observe my emotions, rather than act on them, to avoid creating unwanted karma—sticky situations. I've not always succeeded at this practice, and always paid the price when I haven't, but I've learned to be more aware and found that emotions always cool and shift in time. The cooling-off period creates distance so we can move from the emotional brain to the rational brain and make better-informed, less reactive decisions about how to act. To do this requires tools.

There are many kinds of practitioners, books, and guides to facilitate the healthy release, discussion, and understanding of emotions. Daniel Goleman's classic book *Emotional Intelligence* discusses strategies for defusing anger such as questioning our train of thought and taking long walks. In hypnosis, health coaching, Family Constellations work, and other forms of coaching, bodywork, or therapy, the healthy, nonjudgmental, and safe expression of emotion can lead to a more relaxed and empowered state of mind and body.

For all these reasons, emotion words that are sometimes thought of as negative, such as fear, anger, and sadness, are not negative words in the same way that emotions are not negative. Emotions can be uncomfortable, but allowing ourselves to feel and learn from them, as uncomfortable as that may be, assists us in developing and understanding our humanity.

2. Happiness and Acceptance Words

Even though it's normal to experience a range of emotions, the desire to seek happiness and pleasure is connected to our spiritual and biological survival as individuals and as a species. Sadness has a purpose, but prolonged sadness can isolate a person from their support system. People who live in a state of fear about joblessness may be struggling to survive, with hunger and worry clouding their happiness. Habitually angry people push others away. Happiness is a sign of prosperity, good health, and social connection. When there's enough, when things are going well, we can relax and enjoy life more easily than if we're experiencing difficulties.

On a biochemical level, Candace Pert suggests that the large distribution of opiate receptors throughout our bodies points to our being hardwired for happiness.[13] From a spiritual view, the Dalai Lama also tells us that happiness is innate: "From the moment of birth, every human being wants happiness and does not want suffering."[14] In the United States' Declaration of Independence the words "We hold these truths to be self-evident" (originally written as "sacred and undeniable") are used to describe our human right for the preservation of life, liberty, and the pursuit of happiness. Happiness is sacred to humans.

This is why words like abundance, prosperity, and auspicious give us such positive feelings. They signal safety, bountiful circumstances, good luck, and happiness. In the same way, words like friend, ally, and angel indicate support and cooperation. Of course, abundance and prosperity may be experienced differently from one person to another. Intimate friendship or good meditations are prosperity to one person whereas accumulating money or living a creative life may be prosperity to others. But does happiness depend on life circumstances such as abundance? Perhaps it's possible to cultivate happiness in all life situations through a radical acceptance of whatever happens.

After seeing many practitioners who didn't know how to help me, I had to crawl into my own healing cave and fully accept my situation in order to figure out what to do next. In his book, *Healing Words,* Larry Dossey calls this path "The Formula of No Formula."[15] Inside this cave, it's possible to hear your own intuitive voice and know what to do next. What unfolded for me was a life transformation I would not have experienced had my condition cleared up sooner. I traveled to various parts of the country to work with unique specialists, began writing again, learned nature photography, acquired additional coaching skills in health coaching and hypnosis to adjust my career path, and took early retirement. I didn't decide these changes in advance, but rather followed the unfolding to what felt right, healing, and necessary. The losses I experienced birthed an opportunity to reconfigure old dreams and time to develop budding interests. As Dossey says, "the willingness to experience pain, the *acceptance* of unpleasantness, can transform them into something else."[16] Into something positive.

Another person I spoke with about the role of emotions in golden words echoed that sentiment: "The words we use help us process these emotions and make sense of ourselves and those around us. I find if I document both positive and negative emotions through words it helps me appreciate both sides. Feeling the negative words then propels me to the positive side. That feels empowering."

Emotions aren't always comfortable, but they make us human and can't be ignored. Our emotions can be a guiding light to empowerment and seeing both sides of a situation once we make friends with them. Accepting our humanity in all of its emotional tones brings a peace of its own, whereas fighting against them creates an ongoing battle that can't be won. It's best to dive into the situation, and accept our emotions, as well as the life circumstances that trigger them, which invites a flow we can learn to swim in. In this surrendered state, we can dive for treasures and swim toward a new destination with unforeseen, but positive possibilities. Emotions may feel uncomfortable at times, but managed well, can be positive and empowering.

3. Taking Control and Mastery Words

During my first year of classroom teaching, I had a student who introduced me to the concept of learned helplessness. This six-year-old boy had learned to give up when the going got tough because other people did everything for him when he got frustrated. He came to believe he couldn't do anything on his own, from tying his shoes to learning to read, and gave up before getting started. When presented with a task, he would say, "I can't." With an *I-can't* attitude, this boy robbed himself of building skills and inner strength.

Martin Seligman, who coined the term "learned helplessness," emphasizes that how we talk to ourselves about what's happened (our explanatory style) determines whether we give up or continue on. A pessimistic style feeds helplessness, but optimism stops it. A pessimist imagines the worst will happen and last a long time, but an optimist realizes it's transitory and resolvable. Optimists are not defeated by defeat. They believe they have control to master the situation.[17] Optimists step up their game and embody golden words like autonomous, resilient, and empowered.

From tying your shoes when you're six to picking yourself up after losing a job, telling yourself that you can do it will bring you to the finish line, as opposed to the pessimist, who sits down at the starting gate.

4. Physical Health Words

Our physical health is the foundation of our life. For this reason, when psychologist Abraham Maslow developed a hierarchy to describe human needs, he placed our basic physical and biological needs such as food, air, water, and sleep at the foundation.

To meet these needs, we've been provided with life-giving oxygen, food sources, and shelter resources on our planet. Without Earth's resources, we wouldn't be here. The ways we use and care for them—including methods for farming land, utilizing natural resources, recycling, and protecting the Earth—all support our physical health and well-being. The Earth also provides us with landscapes where we can exercise our bodies and feed our spirits. This results in golden words such as food, water, health, fitness, exercise, healing, medicine, doctor, nurse, and Earth-related words like conservation, farming, and ecology.

Maslow's hierarchy implies that if we're dying of thirst, we can't do much else but search for a way to survive. Once we have a way to take care of our survival and related medical needs, no matter how meager or lush, then we have time to meet our higher needs. The same is true in our emotional life, where the fear of not being able to take care of our survival needs can prevent us from attending to higher needs. For example, a person worried about having enough money to cover the rent might feel pushed to find work at the expense of fulfilling a perceived life purpose. According to the hierarchy, only once we meet our survival needs do we have the psychological space to pursue our social needs and life purpose.

Although Maslow's hierarchy provides a tidy way to organize human needs, he didn't believe a strict order had to be followed. Each person prioritizes their needs in a way that's unique to their own values. We all must meet our physical needs in order to survive, but as you'll see in the discussions that follow, there's no set order to follow to pursue your life purpose or other aspects of the hierarchy.

5. Social Words

Although the hierarchy separates different types of needs, love and belonging are intertwined with our safety and survival. We've learned that babies, as well as children and adults, don't thrive when they aren't touched. We know that people who are bullied have been driven to suicide. People go to great lengths to find belonging, starting in childhood where groups are often identified by their predominant interests, creating cliques such as the athletes, the artists, the nerds, and so on. Feeling left out can be emotionally painful, but being left out can be dangerous to an individual when the group they're part of is connected to their survival. Being included ensures the individual has the support she needs to function, survive, and have a chance to thrive within the community. Some golden social words include community, friendship, ally, belonging, and connected.

6. Life Purpose Words

Finding meaning and purpose in our lives is uniquely human. Some people do that within the conventional norms of society, but Maslow believed that people engaged in *self-actualization*—the term he used for fulfilling one's life-purpose—are not bound too tightly by social norms. Instead, they focus on problems outside of themselves, are spontaneous, creative, and may have more peak experiences than others. This implies there's no need to fit in to make a difference. In fact, you may "fit out," a term Joshua Rosenthal, founder of the Institute for Integrative Nutrition, coined to describe people whose beliefs and lifestyles fall outside the mainstream.

There are other exceptions to living according to the order of the hierarchy. For example, some individuals don't fulfill their survival needs before their self-actualization needs. A well-known example is J. K. Rowling, who wrote her first Harry Potter book when she was struggling to survive. Another high-profile example is Neale Donald Walsch, who wrote *Conversations with God* when he was unemployed and living on the streets. They demonstrate that we can pursue creative, life purpose goals no matter what our financial circumstances. It wasn't easy for them, but they made their choices possible.

Some golden life purpose words include fulfillment, achievement, victory, career, profession, vocation, and self-actualization.

7. Uplifting Words

Following these positive needs in the hierarchy are peak experiences. Maslow placed peak experiences alongside self-actualization in his hierarchy of needs, though these experiences aren't limited to people who are self-actualized. Maslow defined peak experiences using many golden words and phrases such as "profound moments of love, understanding, happiness, or rapture, when a person feels more whole, alive, self-sufficient and yet a part of the world, more aware of truth, justice, harmony, and goodness."[18] These peak experiences include a long stream of golden words, which I've categorized as *uplifting* words.

The uplifting states my clients enjoy such as joyful, blessed, love, peaceful, free, and empowered echo the peak experiences Maslow talks about at the top of his hierarchy. They're also the feelings we're after when we run long distances, travel to places of natural beauty, connect with people we love, pursue our life purpose, meditate with the goal of experiencing our Higher Self, pray, or use self-hypnosis to relax.

If you love nature, uplifting words might include wondrous, breathtaking, awe-inspiring, peaceful, gorgeous, vast, and panoramic. If you work in the medical fields or experience a challenge, uplifting words might include hope, optimism, healing, and courage. Uplifting words to a spiritual person might include angels, blessings, courage, faith, and trust. Uplifting words can be general, but also specific and related to the interests and vocations that bring you great joy.

8. Ways of Knowing Words: Visual, Auditory, Kinesthetic, Olfactory, Gustatory, Intuitive

We each have preferred sensory modes for taking in and processing information. These are known as learning styles or learning modalities and impact our word and lifestyle preferences. Some of these sensations are discussed further in the metaphor section below.

A kinesthetic person, who's tuned into sensation and learns by doing, may be comforted by words such as silky, soft, floating, and solid, but dislike words like sharp or pointy. They enjoy remembering how something feels on their body, such as warm or cool water or a silk scarf. Kinesthetic people also tend to talk slowly.

Visual people have vivid imaginations and easily see mental pictures and colors. They can be comforted by certain colors and imagery. They tend to talk fast.

An auditory person enjoys sound words. My auditory clients who suffer from sleeplessness are often helped by a white noise machine, which masks night noises that sometimes keep them awake.

If you're olfactory-oriented, naming scent words, herbs, or flowers can trigger a deep feeling of relaxation or a strong feeling of aversion. I like to imagine the scent of orange blossoms because I lived in Arizona for several years. The intoxicating scent left a strong memory.

Most people will salivate at the mention of food and experience cravings. But if you're highly gustatory, imagining the taste of something in your mouth and enjoying that taste, without eating it, may actually reduce the judgment you have about a taboo food. That's because the imagination and memory can provide a satisfying experience, and give you the time it takes to resist actually eating that food. The mastery of overcoming a craving in this way can be highly satisfying. With the letter Y, I've provided a tool that takes you through this process.

When I describe the sea as part of a hypnosis session, one of my kinesthetic clients frequently describes everything she feels, from the wind on her face to the feeling of pebbles on her feet. My visual clients see the varying shades of blue in the sea and sky, the sun glittering on the water, and occasionally find items of interest on the beach. An auditory client hears the waves and sounds of seagulls. A gustatory person tastes the salt air and recollects the taste of foods they ate at a beach. An olfactory person smells the fresh air and other incidental aromas on the beach like hot dogs or suntan lotion.

As you read these descriptions of the seashore, which of the modalities appeal to you? Chances are you're attracted to more than one, since we're complex, multi-dimensional beings. Though we have preferences, we use all of our senses. The fact is some of you reading this book may not be drawn to the sea at all. Each person is different, which is why I always ask my clients to describe what's relaxing to them before we work together.

In addition to knowing through our senses, we can know something intuitively. Intuitive knowledge mirrors our sensory knowledge, but the information doesn't always come to us physically. We hear intuitively through our spiritual ears (clairaudience), see intuitively through our spiritual eye (clairvoyance), and sense information and emotions through touch or feelings (clairsentience). You might also smell something not quite right when you're in an uncomfortable situation, and some people even taste something off in food that's been prepared by an unhappy person.

Words that support different ways of knowing validate how we experience the world around us, teach us that everyone has their own unique blend of perceptual abilities, and open us up to new perspectives.

9. Metaphors, Imagery, Stories, and Play Words

Using metaphors, imagery, stories, and play bypasses the critical mind, which might otherwise resist the suggestions you'd like to incorporate. For example, when you're trying to fall asleep, the more you tell yourself to do so, the less likely you are to get any rest. In hypnosis, this is called the Law of Reversed Effect. The more you try to force a physiological response, the less likely you are to succeed. Engaging your creative imagination in metaphors, imagery, stories, and play occupies the mind so the body can relax.

I worked with a client to help her sleep better. She mentioned that she slept very well at summer camp as a child. After hearing the story, I wove the sensory details she'd told me of sleeping soundly into her hypnosis session, telling her a story about sleeping soundly. She fell into a deeply relaxed state, then took home several auditory and visual tools to assist herself at home in easily falling asleep.

Everyone has his own way of falling asleep. Some people like the feeling of lying on a large towel on the warm sand or relaxing in a Jacuzzi. Other people go to sleep easily with a slow body scan. For people who have trouble sleeping, recollecting sensory experiences can create a powerful lullaby for the mind so the body-mind can get some rest. Remembering that sleep is a natural function that the body innately knows how to do can also help.

I have another client whose emotional goal is to experience peace. Peace is an abstract word so the mind and body grope for meaning—perhaps a memory of a person or place triggers the feeling of peace. For this client, it was a reservoir of peace that worked for her. She can float in the still waters of a reservoir of peace and *feel* at peace. Another client enjoys the rush of a waterfall of light cascading over her to shift her state. The waterfall triggers joy and relaxation for her. Another client likes the image and sound of a door closing to trigger relaxation. He leaves his concerns behind that closed door. Metaphor words and imagery help us create tangible, positive experiences from abstract ideas.

Children are very good at using their imaginations in play. In my children's yoga classes, kids drift into meditation quickly and fly off on their magic carpets, blue stars, or other enchanted vehicles to visit magical realms and learn from wise guides. We travel into forests where wish-fulfilling jewels grow on trees and doors open to other dimensions. When we grow up we're taught to put our childhood play behind us and join an adult reality, but our creative imagination is an important tool for cultivating what we want to experience, whether it's feelings in our body or in our physical reality.

I worked with a client who wasn't sure what she wanted. She enjoyed her work, but felt that her life had been about taking care of other people's needs, so she had fallen out of touch with her own dreams and life purpose. Once in hypnosis, we asked her subconscious and her spiritual resources to provide information about her life purpose. She started her session with a vision of being at a waterfront and soon a cottage rose up out of the water and stood on a sand dune. Stepping-stones appeared to float on the water, providing her with a path to the cottage. In front of the structure were two guides, people who were her teachers in movement and ceramics courses. They were teaching her how to play and enjoy the sensory experiences of what she loved.

In this realm of play, she had access to the powerful energy of transformation and felt completely present. She could use energy to mold clay, affect her students, and enjoy her own meditation. Sitting at the table were some pointy-nosed spectacled people who looked judgmental. Her movement teacher said, "Oh, they need to learn to play. Give it a whirl!" encouraging her to experiment and play. She wanted to deliberately fit playtime into her life, yet she realized play could not be scheduled because its nature is free and flows through everything all the time. With that understanding, she suddenly understood how to incorporate play into her daily activities as well as her artwork and meditation. She could play *all* the time.

Our subconscious mind is a rich source of creativity, imagery, intuition, and archetypes. Our subconscious mind loves to play, pretend, and imagine. Playing with metaphors and imagery puts you in touch with a powerful force for creation, transformation, and insight. Give it a whirl— and play like a mad scientist!

10. Laughter Words

In his well-known book *Anatomy of an Illness,* Norman Cousins writes about how he used laughter as a healing agent, successfully combating a rare, life-threatening illness. Though we're not always in the mood to laugh when life gets tough, a sense of humor can interrupt a negative feeling and bring an unexpected flow of endorphins. As an educator, I learned from David Sousa's work connecting brain research and learning that laughter also provides more oxygen to the brain and bloodstream, reduces feelings of stress, moderates blood pressure, creates rapport, and increases memory retention and recall.[19] Laughter reminds us that everything is okay.

I have a client who loves to laugh. Despite the life challenges she faces, she always finds the humor in a situation during her sessions. She doesn't laugh at the expense of other people; rather, she's able to see her life situations with curiosity and an open-mind. Because of this, she gains insights that make her laugh. Laughter, and a new way of seeing things, releases the tension of her challenges.

I think we'd all agree that, as the saying goes, laughter is often the best medicine, even if it is inappropriate at times. As Ecclesiastes 3:1 says: "There is a time for everything, and a season for every activity under the heavens." Sometimes healing tears fall, at other times we laugh our way to happiness.

Eight Principles for Crafting Effective Mantras, Affirmations, and Autosuggestions

You, yourself, as much as anybody in the entire universe,
deserve your love and affection.

BUDDHA

Mantras, Affirmations, and Autosuggestions: What's the Difference?

Mantras, affirmations, and autosuggestions have grown in popularity over the last 50 years because they essentially alter your mental-emotional state, which creates a positive ripple effect in your life. But what's the difference between mantras, affirmations, and autosuggestions? Does it matter which one you use and how you use it?

Knowing the historical origins and intentions for mantras, affirmations, and autosuggestions helps to explain how they've been used effectively in different contexts. They're different, though nowadays they're frequently jumbled together and used interchangeably. Still, they can each be used in a variety of ways to create positive change. Looking at these words together will keep us on the same page and using the same language.

Mantras

A mantra is a word or phrase used in meditation as a point of focus to aid in concentration. A spiritual teacher offers the student a mantra to quiet the mind and connect to the Self, whose nature is expansive, peaceful, blissful, and free. A Sanskrit mantra is considered sacred, the words born from the experience of the thing itself. As the mantra steadies the mind, our true nature, which has been there all along, becomes evident.

When I was given a mantra, the meditation teacher referred to it as "chaitanya," which means alive with consciousness. Repetition of a chaitanya mantra offers the student a direct experience of the mantra's transcendent reality. Mantra repetition also helps regulate the breath, which can draw you into a meditative state. We repeat a mantra so it will make a home within ourselves, and, throughout all of life's ups and downs, provide an anchor of peace and equanimity. In the same way, *all* words are alive with consciousness. When we use any word, we harvest the fruit of its feeling-meaning.

If you're a meditator and seek to experience the Self, you probably use a mantra or other focusing technique to still your mind. That peaceful, joyful state of inner freedom you experience doesn't depend on outer circumstances. The mantra acts like a boat that carries you to those higher states within, but if you're living in this world, you'll have to think and speak about other things. This is where positive words come in. Swami Satchidananda, founder of Integral Yoga, calls it a trick: "We use the trick of developing certain positive thoughts while removing negative ones."[1] We tell the mind, which wants to create thoughts, to go ahead, but to create thoughts that don't bring pain. In this way, we make friends with our mind.

Though mantras are considered, historically, to be sacred vehicles to transcendent spiritual experiences, the word "mantra" has caught on and is frequently used to describe an everyday word or phrase that supports other types of accomplishments. Diana Nyad, who at age 64 became the first person to swim from Cuba to Florida without a protective cage, created her own mantra to help her cross those treacherous waters. As she reported to CBS News during her post-swim interviews, her mantra was "find a way." [2] And find a way, she did. Despite four previous failures, the mortal dangers of her task, and her age, she completed the swim successfully.

"Find a way" may not be a mantra in the Sanskrit sense of the word, but when our intention becomes intensely focused on achieving something specific, the repetition of the phrase anchors us to our intention, which can become as powerful and self-fulfilling as a mantra. The power of self-talk can take us to many destinations, depending on where we focus our attention.

Affirmations

I recall the flourishing popularity of affirmations in the 1980s, due in large part to Louise Hay's work, including her book *You Can Heal Your Life*. Unlike mantras, affirmations don't always have a spiritual intent, but can be repeated to create a specific feeling about the self or to reach a goal, just like a mantra does. Affirmations also tend to be written in longer sentences than the mantras we repeat when meditating. The mantra, "find a way," could become the affirmation, "I find a way to reach my goal easily and quickly."

Suggestions and Autosuggestions

Suggestions come in many forms. In the course of a normal conversation, especially if someone presents a problem or a complaint, people will offer suggestions to show support. Some suggestions might be indirect such as, "Have you tried the x, y, z diet approach? It worked for me."

Other suggestions are more direct like, "Tell your boyfriend/girlfriend/friend you won't put up with that behavior." Or, "You look really good in blue, you should wear it more often."

Veiled suggestions come from television and magazines: drive this car and you'll be sexier; eat this food and you'll have more fun; take this medication and you'll feel better; go on this vacation and you'll be happy. Some suggestions may be useful and wanted, while others may be unhelpful and unwelcome.

If you believe a suggestion might be helpful, you may consciously decide to accept it and act on it. At other times, you may not realize you've accepted the suggestion, and you act on it unconsciously. Either way, you've taken in the suggestion and made it your own, which changes the suggestion into an autosuggestion—a suggestion you give to yourself. If you reject the suggestion, either consciously or unconsciously, it *doesn't* become an autosuggestion.

In addition to the suggestions we get—and sometimes adopt—from other people, we give ourselves autosuggestions all the time. One type of autosuggestion might be a direct, but neutral reminder, "Note to self: Remember to turn the sprinkler off before going to bed." Other autosuggestions might be critical or positive, but also subtle. For instance, changing your clothes three times because you feel insecure about your appearance is likely the result of subtle, unconscious autosuggestions. Making healthy, nourishing dietary choices can also come from autosuggestions. The underlying message behind your actions gives you information about the autosuggestion and the belief system you've adopted, either consciously or unconsciously.

You're also giving yourself autosuggestions when you coach yourself through a situation, like rehearsing a conversation you'll have with a specific individual or giving yourself a positive nudge such as, "Must remember to sit up straight, breathe into my belly, and remain confident during my annual performance review." The fact is we all talk to ourselves. What do we say to ourselves and how do we take in those ideas? Are we critical but compassionate listeners?

Unlike in daily life, where a mix of desirable and undesirable suggestions flow in, suggestions in a hypnosis session focus on supporting and facilitating the client's desired change. Some hypnotists interview their clients to obtain helpful information for creating effective suggestions; other hypnotists use tested scripts to support a client's goal. In both contexts, suggestions are agreed-upon and based on the specific goal. Appropriate positive suggestions are important because, as you'll learn in "Hypnosis: Fact and Fiction," the power of hypnosis lies in the suggestible state where significant and desirable shifts can take place.

Emile Coué (1857–1926), a French psychologist and pharmacist, is the father of autosuggestion. He developed the general, well-known autosuggestion, "Every day in every respect, I'm getting better and better."[3] He used this phrase, along with remedies and other hypnosis processes, to treat his patients. Patients then adopted the phrase for themselves.

There are different points of view on whether the word *autosuggestion* is technical vocabulary referring only to self-hypnosis or if anything we say to ourselves is an autosuggestion. Since we don't always know when we're in a suggestible state, I think of any self-talk as autosuggestion—especially if we repeat it to ourselves often.

Your autosuggestions may be positive or destructive. In this book, the focus is on positive autosuggestions, which I also refer to as positive or golden *self-talk*. Since I'm referring to anything we repeat to ourselves as an autosuggestion, mantras and affirmations fall into this category as well. For all practical purposes, mantras, affirmations, and autosuggestions are *all* self-talk. When they're positive, they're positive self-talk. Positive self-talk is golden.

The eight principles in this chapter will help you craft effective mantras and affirmations you can use for your own golden autosuggestions.

PRINCIPLE 1

Think Big, but Count the Small Changes

When I was a child, my parents gave me a savings account passbook. My dad taught me the saying, "A penny saved is a penny earned." At the time, a gumball cost a penny and the drugstore had bins of penny candy. I would save my pennies so I could buy a 25-cent candy bar or go to a 50-cent movie. When I had saved more than enough, I could give something to charity at Sunday school.

These days, a penny doesn't seem like much—a single gumball costs a quarter—but accumulated pennies still make up a dollar, 10 dollars, 100 dollars, and a million dollars. It's the same way with personal change. Small changes accumulate into bigger and bigger changes until one day you've accomplished a tremendous goal such as losing weight, completing a graduate degree, healing from an injury, becoming a master carpenter, painting a landscape, or writing a book.

Here's an example of how it works in practice. In hypnosis-coaching sessions, I learn about my clients' stories and find out what they'd like to experience differently. (Learn more about hypnosis in "Hypnosis: Fact and Fiction.") In hypnosis, when a person's conscious mind relaxes deeply, resources from their subconscious and intuition step into the conversation. Each session results in a positive movement toward finding solutions and revising their story. Depending on the client's ultimate goal, success may require a series of sessions, with client practice and participation in between sessions, to reach their larger goals—just like saving up pennies for riches.

For example, it might be possible for a person with a sugar addiction to break it after one session, unless the eating habit connects to other issues that need to be addressed. One of my clients who wanted to cut down on her sugar intake talked about what was happening when her sugar issue started. It turned out she'd lost a family member and began to mourn, turning to sweets to assuage her grief. After one session, she felt more in control of her sugar intake.

As a child, another client had always felt close to her mom when they baked cookies together. She made cookies for her own family and ate more than she wanted to because the ritual helped her feel close to the people she cared most about. In hypnosis, she recalled a memory of her mom that had the closeness she longed for but without the cookies. During subsequent sessions, she identified other situations in her life that triggered her desire for sugar. This empowered her to use memories, autosuggestions, and self-awareness to sweeten those areas of her life as she gradually reduced her sugar intake.

Finally, some clients want to reduce, but not give up sugar. For some people this may work, but for many people it doesn't because sugar is comparable in some ways to addictive drugs.[4] When clients learn about the powerful effect sugar has on the brain's reward system, most of them are eager to find different rewards, cultivate healthier eating habits, and be free of sugar.

Count your pennies.
All big bills are made up
of small change.

PRINCIPLE 2
Maintain the Big Picture in the Present Tense

If you want to be happy tomorrow, you'll always be waiting for tomorrow. Of course, you may have long-term goals that can't be achieved in one day; so in some ways you're working toward a series of tomorrows. For example, if successfully earning a higher education degree is your goal, this will take a number of years, depending on your area of study. For success in school, your present tense affirmation might be: "I am a successful student earning exam scores of 85 percent and higher."

You can also build the bigger picture—your tomorrows—into your affirmation. For example: "I'm a successful student and graduate, living my life purpose as a (business executive, teacher, therapist, etc.), impacting people's lives positively, and making X dollars each year." Your current focus goes toward being a successful student who's taking courses, writing papers, and doing the readings, but you're still imagining yourself in the bigger picture earning your diploma and making money in a successful professional career. You can break down any goal or set of goals to create this type of phrase for yourself.

Staying in the present tense reminds you of what you're doing now and how it connects to and facilitates your ultimate, larger reward. Goals with incremental rewards and bigger ones at the end are like the proverbial carrot leading the horse forward.

Staying in the present tense
while maintaining the big picture
is a gift that keeps on giving.

PRINCIPLE 3

Create Believable Goals and Adjust as Needed

How big do you dream? What do you do in the face of upsets? Creating believable goals that you're free to adjust as you progress can make the difference between false starts and staying the course.

Believability

Believability varies from person to person. You'll have to ask yourself what's believable to you. When I was at the height of pain after my accident, it was hard to believe I'd ever be pain-free again. Yet I knew I would be because of several encouraging dreams that anchored me to the belief in my body's ability to heal. Nonetheless, attaining a pain-free state took small steps and believable goals along the way. If you have physical pain that prevents you from doing heavy exercise, you can't make a goal to jog next week, but you might set a goal to walk for a few minutes each day, then gradually build your activity level as you improve. As you can see, this principle is closely tied to Principle 1, thinking big but counting the small changes. Small steps are more likely to be believable, and this belief is crucial to gaining ground. As you accomplish the smaller goals, you'll set bigger ones. Setting believable, incremental goals adds up.

Estimates and Adjustments

Just because you set a believable goal doesn't mean you'll reach it in the time you've allotted. Estimate what you think is possible, then go for it. If you reach your goal, continue forward. If you estimated too high, adjust accordingly. Be easy on yourself, and celebrate the small stuff, as you take steps forward at your own pace.

I was at the gym for 12–15 hours a week prior to my bike accident. After the accident, I couldn't take a walk for almost two years. I knew I wanted to ride my bike and jog again, but I didn't know how long it would take to get there. At 22 months I could take walks, at three years I could lift light weights (which was very painful at first!), and at four years I rode my bike. Within five years I was walking for hours out in nature carrying heavy camera equipment on a waist-belt and in my hands. I jogged a couple of times and realized I didn't care much for that type of exercise anymore so I adjusted my goals.

In the same way, you may have an *ultimate* goal that you want to attain, but as you proceed, you might change your mind. I saw this happen with a few students in my teacher education programs who always wanted to be teachers, but once they were in the classroom, they didn't enjoy the day-to-day lifestyle. It's the same with anything you dream about. The reality of your dream may not be what you thought it would be. If it's not, it's okay to adjust your goals. Experimenting and playing at what brings you joy is at the heart of living.

Think big, write believable
goals for the present, and adjust
your goals as you proceed.

PRINCIPLE 4
Take Advantage of Habit, Repetition, and Emotion

The neuroscience of brain plasticity demonstrates that although we may have habit patterns we aren't happy with, we can take our lives into our own hands and make conscious changes for the better. We do this through repetition and strong emotion.

Habits

We've built our lives and habit patterns over a number of years. In my early years of education, I learned how children learn and acquire habits from Harry Wong, a prominent educator who writes and lectures internationally. Wong cites the work of educator Madeline Hunter, which says that for a child to learn something *new*, the behavior must be repeated about 8 times, but if an old behavior must be *unlearned* and replaced with new behavior, it must be repeated about 28 times. About 20 repetitions eliminate the old behavior and 8 repetitions install the new behavior.[5]

Now, I've known children and adults who learned the very first time. Children are quite suggestible through their teen years so they take in information very quickly, especially if they connect emotionally or through their favored sensory modes. I also have clients who've quit smoking, overcome sleeplessness, or found inner peace in an area of their life within one to three hypnosis-coaching sessions. But for others, especially those with deeply rooted habits, setting up new behavior patterns may take time and repetition. When we realize that transforming habits takes time, we can be more patient with ourselves—and others.

Creating and changing habits is also rooted in neuroscience, which has an explanation for how habits take shape in our brains. Hebbs' Law, named after Donald Hebbs, a Canadian psychologist, refers to how input to the brain sets up firing patterns among neurons. The more we repeat habitual activities and thoughts, the bigger and stronger the corresponding brain map grows. This is how *practice makes permanent.* It may be what you want, and therefore perfect, too. But if it's not, neuroplasticity studies show that we can change our brains through practicing new thoughts and experiences, especially if they're invested with strong emotion. Repetition of new habits modifies our old brain maps.

Old dogs can learn new tricks.

Emotions Rule

Remember our discussion about fear in "From Serene to Silly: What Makes a Word *Golden?*" Joseph LeDoux taught us in the early days of brain research that the emotional processing hub in the brain forms associations between outside stimuli, regardless of whether they feel good or distressing, and "stamps in those experiences" and connections. This means we best recall intense emotional experiences. If we want to replace the feelings of those experiences with different ones, we have to stamp in new memories with the positive feelings we want in our lives. It's easier to remember trauma, but with focus you can remember pleasant experiences and develop new, good memories, too.

For instance, after my bike accident, it took me four years to regain the physical and emotional comfort to get back on my bike and ride through the accident site. First, I rehearsed the bike rides in my mind, reminding myself of the joy of riding a bike. I had many happy memories to call on for support. I also had flashbacks of my near-fatal ride, but they decreased in intensity over time. I took safety precautions, and I consciously looked around my environment to prove to myself that I was, indeed, safe and in the present moment. I still remember the accident, but I get on my bike now without thinking about it, except in gratitude for being able to ride and enjoy my life. Combining mental-emotional rehearsal with getting out and making new memories dialed down the trauma of the previous bike ride.

Transforming emotionally intense experiences not only takes practice, but practice with emotion. Just as I rehearsed having fun and feeling safe on each of those subsequent bike rides in order to modify my brain map, you have to feel the mantra or affirmation you're repeating. If you can't bring up the emotion you want, there may be an intermediate step needed such as asking yourself if it's what you really want, modifying the goal if necessary, or feeling an emotion you may be avoiding.

Use the power of your
emotions and mental rehearsal
to create new possibilities.

PRINCIPLE 5
Mind Your Emotional Tone

Have you ever had a boss, lover, or friend who said something cutting, but their smile and delivery disguised the words so it took a minute for your brain to catch up and realize you'd been sliced? The opposite can happen, too. Someone says, "I love you," but for some reason the words don't ring true. You know it from their tone. This is why emotional tone is so important.

If you say to yourself, "Everyday in every respect, I'm getting better and better," but in the back of your mind you're thinking, "Yeah, right. NOT," then chances are you need to change your sentence, make a conscious effort to look for ways your life is improving, or consciously address what's not getting better. Repeating a list of negative thoughts and feelings while repeating your mantra, affirmation, or autosuggestion just strengthens what you want to change. Nonetheless, if a list of what's not going right pops up, that's your opportunity to identify and clear out those obstacles.

On the other hand, if you can use an encouraging or victorious tone when you say to yourself, "Everyday in every respect, I'm getting better and better," while taking the time to reflect on all the ways you're getting better, you create hope and self-empowerment about your continued progress.

Say it like you mean it.

PRINCIPLE 6
Be Affirmative

If you were a *Star Trek* fan, you heard Captain Jean Luc Picard tell his crew members to "make it so," when he asked for a command to be carried out. He never said, "Don't not make it so." In the same way that a captain creates an aura of authority by giving a positive command, it's generally regarded in education, hypnosis, and meditation communities that the subconscious mind follows the positives most successfully.

The example often given in hypnosis is "Don't think of a pink elephant;" in meditation it's "Don't have a monkey-mind." If you tell a child not to slam the door, not to fight, or not to talk out of turn, he or she will not grasp the "not" and will perform the action you hope to prevent. This is because you've only offered an example of what you don't want. This simple truth suggests that we avoid negative statements to prevent continually recreating what we don't want. Conversely, stating something in the affirmative leads us to what we do want.

Replacing a negative statement requires crafting a positive statement to take its place, such as *please raise your hand to talk, let's work this out with words, and please close the door quietly.* In hypnosis, pain is reframed positively as discomfort. Instead of getting rid of discomfort, we work toward gaining comfort. We move toward a positive state by increasing what is beneficial rather than trying to reduce what we don't want. Think of it this way: creating a new job entails imagining and working toward what you want to do as opposed to complaining about your misery. Creating positive statements supports movement toward the positive.

Make it positive
and make it so.

PRINCIPLE 7
Use "I Statements"

"I statements" use the subject *I*, as in "I will," "I do," "I am." When using golden self-talk, you're talking to and about yourself, which requires using "I statements."

However, many people consider focusing on themselves to be wrong, selfish, or narcissistic. The problem with not focusing on yourself, though, is that you put your happiness in other people's hands. You have to know what you want out of life to create that. Otherwise, you could end up floating aimlessly from one thing to another, your choices could get lost in the self-sacrifice of living out someone else's agenda, or you could become paralyzed with indecision.

You also can't control what other people do. Therefore, your mantras and affirmations have to focus on you because that's what's in your control. You can't control who wants to be your partner, who wants to hire you for a job, or who wants to be your friend. If you want those things in your life, please use the other principles, monitor what happens, and adjust as necessary.

Of course, you can negotiate the language of a mantra or affirmation with your partner, team, friend, or someone else if you'd like to create something together. But when it comes to creating something on your own, it's all about you.

It's okay to take care of yourself.

PRINCIPLE 8
Keep a Journal

When you keep track of your goals and progress, you empower yourself to count the small changes, can be aware of when redirection is needed to adjust and reach those goals, and look for patterns of success. You have the power to speak and write yourself into someone who succeeds at what you want to accomplish, or, you can give that power to someone else and drift through life with no particular goals in mind. By keeping track of your progress, you also keep yourself accountable to the goals you're working toward. This is how you become the cheerleader of your own victory.

Be the author of your
story's plot line, revisions,
and happy ending.

III

Hypnosis: Fact and Fiction

The mind is everything.
What you think, you become.

BUDDHA

People have turned to positive words in the form of affirmations, mantras, and autosuggestions for centuries to replace those uncomfortable ideas and feelings that disrupt their happiness. Using the trance state, you can more easily shift those beliefs and experiences than by will alone.

Yet many of the people I talk to about hypnosis and trance states express common misconceptions that arise from media and entertainment. They've seen cartoons where the characters' bulging eyes are swirling in hypnotic spirals, their arms held out straight ahead like zombies, performing outrageous actions at the hypnotist's command. These caricatures of hypnosis are borne from stage entertainment, where the intention is to create an aura of power and magic. Good stage hypnotists do know how to provide a level of entertainment that appears magical. I won't divulge their secrets because you can read about them online.

I believe the comical but preposterous cartoons associated with entertainment hypnosis have slowed down the acceptance of hypnosis as a valuable method in the mind-body toolkit, where it belongs alongside mindfulness, meditation, exercise, nature, and healthy eating. The power of the mind does have a magical quality, but what appears to be magical has a scientific foundation. Understanding the science of hypnosis will help you appreciate the power of your mind and begin to understand the magic right inside yourself.

It's important to know that a hypnotist can't make you do anything you wouldn't normally do or don't want to do. Moreover, in an office setting, the hypnotist has a very clear intention: to help you feel better and reach your goals. With your well-being in mind, the hypnotist and you discuss your goals and concerns in advance. The hypnotist can then design appropriate and desirable suggestions in regard to your goals. This discussion is important because it gives the hypnotist information she needs to provide you with a successful session. (Not all hypnotists work this way; some work with well-tested scripts, which can also be effective.) The main point being that a good hypnotist, in an office setting, is a guide and facilitator, with your best interests at heart.

I believe that one of the greatest benefits of hypnosis is being able to access your intuitive wisdom, a skill that's much needed in today's society, where so many healing modalities, diets, and self-help books offer competing theories. As the world becomes more global and visibly connected, we are also faced with more choices as old barriers fall away. To find our way around these choices, it's important for us to develop and trust our own inner guidance. When I began studying intuitive processes in the mid 1980s, I was fortunate to learn from Sonia Choquette. She made the point that anyone could access their own intuitive wisdom. It's your birthright.

I agree. When you tune into your own intuitive wisdom, you retrieve information that's already inside you. This builds confidence in your own ability to access resources and make important life decisions. We're all naturally intuitive, but accessing our intuitive and subconscious resources can be facilitated in hypnosis.

Even people who are interested and open to hypnosis wonder if they can be hypnotized. The fact is you *have* been hypnotized to one degree or another because you're in and out of hypnotic trance throughout the day. As a child you were suggestible, taking in ideas and beliefs from others about who you are, then living out those beliefs.

We're also in a trance state when we stare into space in a momentary daydream, stare at the TV or a book and soon feel the characters are real, or stare out at the road and drive somewhere without remembering how we got there. When we go to bed at night and wake up in the morning, we drift between waking and sleeping. During this in-between time, images and information arise spontaneously. Sometimes we receive streams of ideas as whole concepts, at times we see loved ones who've passed, or find solutions to problems that seem to come from nowhere. Like the dream I shared in the preface, we may even glimpse our future. Drifting into a trance state is natural.

I hope you noticed that I referred to the hypnotic state as somewhere *between* waking and sleeping because most people think a hypnotized person falls sleep. This misconception arises in part from the name, "hypnosis," which comes from the Greek word meaning "sleep." James Braid, who gave hypnosis its name in the 1840s, thought his patients had gone to sleep. Later he changed the name to *mono-ideaism,* which means mental focus on one idea.[1] This name didn't catch on, but it better defines the hypnosis experience.

One of my clients wondered if she'd been hypnotized because she had expected to fall asleep. She told me that instead, she felt super-aware, super-focused. Her super-awareness was one signal that she was in a hypnotic trance. Other people think they fall asleep because when hypnosis is coupled with deep relaxation and you dive deeply into the subconscious and intuitive states, the experiences can be subtle, like a dream.

This dreamlike state can be difficult for some people to recall in detail until they've had more experience toggling between states. But like dreams, the images eventually drift away. Also, in a typical hypnosis session, a person will move from deeper to lighter states throughout the session so may feel as if they're in the sleep state at times. In fact, some people *do* fall asleep after entering a deep, relaxing trance state. There are many signs of hypnosis, which not only vary from person to person, but may be different each time a person experiences hypnosis.

It actually doesn't matter if you remember what happens in hypnosis. The hypnotist is speaking to your subconscious mind so that what you'd like to feel becomes automatic, natural, and relaxed as opposed to willed, self-conscious, and difficult. Therein lies a key difference between using hypnosis instead of your everyday state of awareness to replace difficult feelings with more helpful ones. For example, if you want to replace a feeling of insecurity with a feeling of confidence, you can try to convince yourself you're confident through constant mental practice, which may be successful eventually, or use hypnosis to relax and absorb the feeling more easily. Subtle shifts that occur in hypnosis may be difficult to remember and pinpoint, but the positive feelings are long lasting.

You're not alone if you think a hypnotic trance sounds similar to meditation, but the goals of each are different. The main goal of meditation is to quiet the mind of thoughts. A sacred mantra is used to carry the meditator to a higher state as represented by the meaning of the mantra, mainly the experience of divine consciousness. In hypnosis, the client may experience divine consciousness, explore their soul purpose, or investigate turning points, but a person may have less lofty, yet important goals such as releasing food cravings, overcoming fears, reducing stress, reaching athletic goals, breaking through blocks, increased confidence, improved sleep, reduced pain, deep relaxation, and so on. You can also regress to a memory using hypnosis, which can be a powerful transformative and insightful experience. I've used regression in many circumstances including for exploring the near-death experience. A client of mine wanted to learn more about what had happened to him when he almost died in an accident. His experience of love was so profound, he felt as if he were love itself.

The Science of Hypnosis

In 2014, the Society of Psychological Hypnosis, a division of the American Psychological Association (APA), agreed on a definition of hypnosis that was open-ended enough to invite research about how hypnosis works and its relationship, if any, to the waking state, meditation, yoga, and mindfulness. Like Braid's idea of mono-ideaism, the definition says that hypnosis is "A state of consciousness involving focused attention and reduced peripheral awareness characterized by an enhanced capacity for response to suggestion."[2] Because hypnosis opens us up to suggestion, using hypnosis processes with golden words can create powerful positive changes.

Receiving suggestions during hypnosis has been measured using brain scans. These scans reveal the astonishing power of our creative imagination in trance, one of the greatest benefits of hypnosis. Though this research is still young, studies of the hypnotic state show that we're in variable brain wave states ranging across the beta, alpha, theta, and delta states. In hypnosis, brain waves are smoothed, the right hemisphere of our brain is more active, and our attention is more focused.[3] In this altered state of awareness, we can influence our brains to create changes in perception that show up on brain scans *as if* the experience is happening in reality.

In a dramatic example, a study was done to see whether hypnosis could affect color perception. Researchers learned that "The hypnotic illusion of color induced blood flow change consistent with actually observing color."[4] This means that the patient, because of a hypnotic suggestion, saw in color where there was actually a black and white image. *The brain had registered the hypnotic experience as if it were really happening.*[5] Herbert Spiegel coined a powerful phrase about these results: "Simply believing alters patterns of neural activity that is consciously experienced as seeing. In other words, believing becomes seeing."[6] This principle alone makes hypnosis worth understanding: *You have to believe it to see it, not the other way around, which is what most people think.*

When the person saw color, even though the image was black and white, they were having what's called a positive hallucination. A positive hallucination is seeing something that isn't there; a negative hallucination is not seeing something that is there. Being able to hallucinate during hypnosis can impact your experience dramatically, by either installing something that you want, or removing something (such as warts) that you don't want. Remember, you don't have to see it to believe it. You have to believe it to see it. This is an important principle worth repeating.

Used correctly, hallucinations, stimulated with guided imagery, memories, or other techniques, can have healing effects on our bodies. In Dana Reeve's film, *The New Medicine,* Reeve shows how practitioners use hypnotic hallucination in the form of guided imagery, for relief from stress and pain. The film shows Gary Walco using hypnosis with a patient to illustrate how imagining you're in your favorite vacation spot, while in a state of hypnosis, floods the body with the same feelings as if you're really there. This experience empowered his patient to reduce his pain level. Reducing pain and stress, according to the research shared by Glaser and Kiecoult-Glaser, a husband-and-wife research team, speeds up wound healing. Conversely, too many stress hormones lengthen the amount of time needed to heal.[7]

Hypnosis has many applications. Contemporary celebrities, such as Ellen DeGeneres, have used hypnosis to quit smoking.[8] Other stars have used hypnosis for weight release, more comfortable childbirth, sports performance, and many other purposes.

Hypnosis, Creativity, and Intuitive Inspiration

Many famous people have also tapped the power of hypnosis to access information from the subconscious mind to develop their ideas including Albert Einstein and Sergei Rachmaninoff. No one really knows where this flow of creative inspiration comes from. Some people refer to the creative font as the Muses or guiding angels. Spiritual, religious, and philosophical traditions refer to the source of this information as God, Spirit, the Absolute, All That Is, Cosmic Consciousness, and many other names referred to in my author's note.

It's my personal belief, based on my own out-of-body, near-death experience, that this information comes from the matrix of Spirit that underlies our material experience and takes many forms, including guardian angels, guides, and loved ones who've passed on. I can't prove this scientifically, but many people have experienced it and intuitively sense it. If you've ever had ideas dropped in your lap, you know what I mean. You were probably in a trance state when that happened.

Experience the Power of Words

If you'd like to give yourself a small, personal demonstration of how the power of your self-talk, creative imagination, and memories influence your well-being, mull over a difficult situation in your life for about a minute. Contemplate pain, words of despair, or an unhappy memory and watch the discomfort rise in your body and mind. I actually caution you about trying this because you probably won't feel well if you do. If you decide to try it, see if you can observe the discomfort without judgment. Then reverse the effects by imagining something enjoyable, like a favorite place, a pleasant memory, a hopeful outcome, or a healing experience. Allow the discomfort to recede into the distance as your pleasant feeling grows. Notice how your self-talk, your creative imagination, and your interpretation of life situations influence how you feel and how you decide to proceed with your life.

At the moment of noticing the power of your mind to create your own experience, you wake yourself up from the trance of your unquestioned beliefs. That's when you realize the impact of your mind on your actions and emotions. A colleague, lifelong friend, and retired guidance counselor, Marc Denny, describes it like this:

> It's all about living life internally rather than externally. Most folks have little understanding of self-talk, the thinking process and how thinking directs our actions. I often compare this to watching leaves blow in the wind. We know the leaves are blowing, but we don't see the atmospheric pressure creating the wind thus moving the leaves. The leaves are moving (observable action) directed or influenced by changes in the atmosphere (thinking). If you ask a person why the leaves are moving, most would answer, "Because the wind is blowing." One more observation is crucial, what makes the wind?

When we wake up to the way our thoughts (the wind) influence our lives (the leaves blowing in the wind) in both subtle and dramatic ways, therein lies the opportunity to shift the winds by using our own consciously chosen thoughts and golden words.

It's like a game to notice how this works, though I'll be the first to admit that having a positive or even a neutral outlook, when your dominant reality is not what you want it to be, is a discipline. Much like learning to play a new piece on the piano or incorporating a new habit such as meditation into one's schedule, sometimes we hit the wrong key as we're learning or we can't quiet our mind when we close our eyes. If we keep practicing, we have a chance to succeed, but if we don't try, we'll never get a chance to hear the music or experience the riches within.

The Impact of Hypnosis

When a harsh reality stares you in the face, it can be tempting to sink into cynicism, anger, and despair, then wonder if it's really possible. That's when we're tempted to go back to our former way of thinking that *seeing is believing* instead of *believing is seeing*. At times, riding through those feelings is what's needed to digest an experience and come out the other side full of insights. At other times, we're just practicing habitual, limiting feelings and keep riding them to the bottom because we think they're true.

Do any of us really know what's possible? We see limits broken all the time, so why decide in advance what can or cannot be done? Children teach us how to create possibilities all the time when they play at pretending. They rehearse something they want, until they lose interest or become that. We all know children who played at teacher, then became one; or others who put on plays and became actors. But at times, without help, whether it's the tools of golden words or professional help from a hypnotist, coach, therapist, or medical doctor, crawling out of the hole can be a challenge.

In the moment you find yourself at the bottom, what you say to yourself next will make all the difference in the world between flailing around or standing up, brushing yourself off, and moving on. Which way will your wind blow at that moment? Positive thoughts, feelings, and images, or sometimes just one golden word, can be the key to unlocking a floodgate of improvements: empowering insights, reduction of stress or pain, improved sleep and dietary habits, deep relaxation, a sturdier connection to your intuitive wisdom, and awareness of your spiritual resources. You can browse through the golden words and tools in this book and see which ones help you do that.

Nourishment and support for maintaining a positive mindset also come from observing what role models and heroes say to themselves. Along the way I found a hero whose story fuels my own courage: Elie

Wiesel, the well-known Holocaust survivor, Nobel Peace Prize winner, and bestselling author of *Dawn and Night*. As a tireless peace activist, Wiesel is an exemplar of turning the most deplorable curses into blessings. He embodies courage that we can all draw on for the struggles in our own lives: struggles against our own inner demons, the demons of illness, or ones we encounter in the world around us.

Wiesel also demonstrates by example that cultivating a positive mindset is a personal responsibility and promotes a sense of empowerment, especially in situations where we feel out of control. Having myriad medical issues after my accident might have taken a much worse toll on my mind and body had I not continuously sought out golden words, people, and resources for comfort, inspiration, and healing. The fact that my accident and the subsequent challenges I experienced fundamentally changed for the better the way I think and live seems ironic in a book about golden words. In that sense, what is sometimes felt and perceived as negative, challenging, and even catastrophic can be used as a launching pad for positive, personal, and social transformation.

Even if you don't learn hypnosis, self-hypnosis, or work with a hypnotist, considering the fact that you're in and out of hypnotic states throughout the day, just becoming aware of your own self-talk and modifying it to be more encouraging to yourself can have a profound impact on your life. You can uplift yourself and others with the words you choose. You can also learn to develop your own trance state to amplify your golden words. But whether you're in trance or not, your words are a living and powerful force that create your life. Please choose them carefully.

IV

Ten Steps to Relaxation and Self-Hypnosis

Do not dwell in the past,
do not dream of the future,
concentrate the mind
on the present moment.

BUDDHA

To get the most out of using mantras, affirmations, and autosuggestions, you can ease yourself into a gentle trance. Once you've learned the steps and have found what works best for you, the entire process takes about 20 minutes, though you can spend longer if you have time. Also, when you enter a deep state of relaxation, plan to spend a few minutes bringing yourself back to your waking state slowly and gently.

The first step asks you to prepare an autosuggestion to use in your trance state. Steps 2 through 8 will help you experience a trance state. The ninth will give you guidance immediately after a trance and the tenth aims to help you incorporate this practice into your life. The more you practice, the easier it will become. In my experience, experiencing trance states with a hypnotist makes going into trance easier. Being a regular meditator also makes it easier to go into trance.

STEP 1
Write Your Mantra or Affirmation

You can follow Steps 2 through 8 just to relax, but if you decide to take advantage of the suggestible trance state to give yourself a positive auto-suggestion in the form of a mantra or affirmation, then prepare something in advance that you'd like to suggest to yourself. You can use the "Eight Principles for Crafting Effective Mantras, Affirmations, and Autosuggestions" to help you or just play with the process like a mad scientist. Whatever you decide to suggest to yourself, remember to keep it positive and simple. If you want to feel golden, make it golden.

STEP 2
Make Yourself Comfortable

Find a comfortable place to sit or lie down so you can relax fully. Wearing comfortable clothes is recommended. Turn off your phone and be sure you'll have privacy and quiet for your planned length of time. To fully relax, start by remembering a place in nature that you enjoy. This could be near an ocean, walking along a path in the woods, sitting against a tree or under a waterfall, standing on top of a mountain, looking out onto a vast open plain or the ocean, floating among stars, resting on clouds, or whatever real or whimsical idea comes to mind that works for you. Invite spiritual resources—people and/or guides that bring you direction, support, and comfort—to accompany you.

STEP 3
Set Your Intentions

If you have a prepared statement, look at it before you continue. Set the intention to remember and repeat this statement in trance for your highest benefit. Also, set the intention to wake up refreshed and energized for your next activity in 20 minutes, or for the amount of time you decide to be in trance. If you need to go somewhere soon after this activity, you may want to set a timer in advance in case you drift into deep relaxation. Please choose a gentle sound to bring you back. If you'd like to go to sleep afterward, then set the intention to fall sleep.

STEP 4
Focus on the Blue Jewel

As you relax in your favorite nature setting, close your eyes and shift your gaze up to the point between and just above your eyebrows, which is where your *ajna chakra* (*third eye*) is located. You can imagine a shimmering blue jewel there to help you focus your attention.

The ajna chakra, your sixth chakra, is indigo in color and, as the phrase "third eye" indicates, refers to your inner eye, which sees beyond the physical to the spiritual realms. Focusing upward on your sixth chakra also has the spiritual significance of opening up to your intuitive wisdom.

In the field of hypnosis, Herbert Spiegel developed what he called the "Eye-Roll Test of Hypnotizability," which demonstrated that in about 2,000 cases "the ability to look upward on signal correlates highly (73.9%) with hypnotic trance capacity."[1] He observed that looking upward—just with the eyeballs, not with the head—then closing one's eyes, is what some people do naturally when attempting to focus and fence out distractions, not unlike the concentrated attention and reduced peripheral awareness of hypnosis. This upward gaze, where the colored part of the eye begins to disappear under the lids and the lower whites of the eyes show, is also "associated with alpha rhythms," the attentive but relaxed state of meditative concentration.[2]

For all these reasons, concentrating on a blue jewel as a focal point between and just above your eyebrows will draw you inward, reduce distractions, assist you in connecting to your intuitive wisdom, and aid in the shift to alpha rhythm—an awake, but relaxed state.

STEP 5
Take a Few Soothing Breaths

While gazing at the blue jewel between your eyebrows, take a deep breath in through your nose and hold it for a few seconds. Imagine your breath moving easily through your whole body from head to foot to fingertips. Then gently release your breath fully through your nose or mouth. Imagine all the tension in your mind and body blowing out with your breath. Repeat, taking another deep breath in, holding it for a few seconds, allowing it to be like a magnet for any remaining tension you might feel, then release your breath out of your mouth along with that tension.

On your third breath, imagine breathing in light (this can be white light or any color you like) and allow it to bathe and cleanse every cell of your body from the bottoms of your feet, to the top of your head, and down to your fingertips. Hold that breath for a few seconds, allowing it to fill your entire body with light. Then release that breath through your nose or mouth. As you become aware of your fingertips, allow your shoulders to relax down. Now breathe naturally. You can also think of your breath as warm water, a magical elixir, or anything else that suits you to soothe your body into deep relaxation.

If holding your gaze on the blue jewel becomes uncomfortable at any time, allow your eyes to relax and feel soothed.

STEP 6
Experience Soothing Support

Beginning at your feet, become aware of the support beneath your body and allow yourself to sink into that support. Move slowly and gently up to each body part, first the heels of your feet, then your calves, next your thighs. Allow your hips to sink in fully supported, then your lower back, middle back, and upper back. Let your shoulders release down as you lay aside any burdens you've been carrying. You can imagine placing these burdens in a basket, if you like. Allow your neck to soften, your jaw to relax, your lips to part slightly, and your eyes and scalp to go soft. Your whole body feels heavy and supported, though some people may begin to feel light. For some people, tensing and relaxing each muscle group as you progress through each body part aids in relaxation.

If you enjoy a sensory experience, imagine you're walking into a warm sea, a Jacuzzi, or a bathtub little by little. First your feet and ankles, then your calves and knees, next your thighs and hips are submerged in warm, clear water. Then submerge yourself to your waist, your chest, your neck, arms, and shoulders. Finally, immerse your face and head. Feel the warm water washing away your cares.

Some people like to use a heating pad or a blanket. In my office, I use a far infrared mat with clients who like heat. Experiment to find out what works best for you to become comfortable and relaxed.

STEP 7
Count and Breathe with Ocean Waves

Begin counting backwards from 10 to 1. Count slowly and rhythmically, one count per breath (one breath includes the inhalation and exhalation). Match your breathing to the pace of gentle, rolling ocean waves, which you can imagine hearing, seeing, or just noticing in the background. You can also pace your breathing by thinking about something you like that has a slow, relaxing rhythm, such as a leaf drifting down from a tree in autumn, leaves fluttering in the breeze, sunlight glittering on a lake, or circular ripples expanding in a still pond.

When you've completed the backwards count, slowly walk down a gentle incline into your own beautiful and private place of healing. This could be like a spa, a sanctuary, a temple, your nature place, or another place either real or imagined. Bring your spiritual resources with you.

STEP 8

Repeat Your Autosuggestion

In your relaxed and suggestible state, repeat your autosuggestion, which is your mantra or affirmation. Say it to yourself with love, respect, and trust. Repeat it 10 times using the fingers on both hands to count the repetitions. Keep your pace slow like your breathing, matching the pace of the gentle ocean waves.

Let your statement wash through your entire being, like a breath of light, installing it in each and every cell. Say the statement slowly enough to allow and observe supportive memories, images, feelings, and other information to flow through you while you do this. If you drift off, don't be concerned. When your attention comes back, continue.

STEP 9

Wake up Refreshed, Take a Nap, or Go to Sleep

If you want to take a nap or go to sleep, please do so. Otherwise, when you've completed your 10 repetitions, walk back up the incline from your beautiful healing place to your place in nature. Then gently become aware of your body resting against the surface where you're lying or sitting down. Gradually become aware of your surroundings. These steps will bring you out of self-hypnosis gently and gradually.

Take a few minutes to jot down any ideas or feelings that came to you that you want to remember. In addition to other thoughts and feelings this process could reveal, you might have ideas for refining your mantra or affirmation. After taking notes, move on with your day, pay attention to small golden changes, and trust the flow.

STEP 10
Repeat Daily or When Practical

Everyone has a favorite time to relax. For you it might be morning, late afternoon, or when you're climbing into bed at night. There is no right or wrong time to practice relaxation and self-hypnosis. You can also practice when you're getting a massage or acupuncture, at the dentist, or during another treatment where you're lying or sitting for a while.

The ability to relax, focus yourself on your goals, and use golden self-talk both in self-hypnosis sessions and while you're out living your life, improves with practice. If you want to become a sculptor, it's important to chip away at your sculpture in progress. In the same way, if you want to make a change in yourself, accomplish a goal or improve an area of your life, practicing what you want helps to bring it into focus. Like Michelangelo, you'll gradually reveal the *David* you've been imagining.

Epilogue

There's no such thing as a perfect life—and yet there is. By virtue of our spiritual nature, we're already perfect. At times our lives feel perfect, too. We're in sync, everything makes sense, and we have a sudden epiphany about why something happened the way it did.

Living in the physical world makes us forget our true nature at times. We slosh around through the space-time reality of living in a physical body and some days nothing seems to be going right. We don't see the big picture, we feel like we're in the wrong place at the wrong time, or we experience a heavy emotional load. At times like these, if we can touch the joy at the center of our beings and follow it, we can avoid much of the resentment and regret that might prevent us from fulfilling our highest intentions.

Learning to be in the waves of life, both in the rivers of tears and oceans of joy, is part of the human journey. It's our job to pick up an oar, row through it, and keep on rowing. At times, we'll float in moments of glee, victory, and abiding love. There will also be moments of confusion, vulnerability, and pain—when rowing along feels difficult or impossible. But no matter what happens along the way, if you want to live from the heart, golden words are some of the best company you could keep.

Endnotes

Preface

1. Morris, W. (Ed.). (1975). *The American Heritage Dictionary of the English Language*. Boston: Houghton Mifflin.

Abundant A

1. Shankar, A. (2010, June 14). *Arjuna Passes The Test*. Retrieved from Indian Stories For Children: http://anustoriesforchildren. blogspot.com/2010/06/arjuna-passes-test.html

I. From Serene to Silly

1. Ekman, P., Friesen, W. V., O'Sullivan, M., Diacoyanni-Tarlatzis, I., Krause, R., Pitcairn, T., ...Tomita, M. (1987). Personality processes and individual differences: Universals and cultural differences in the judgments of facial expressions of emotion. *Journal of Personality and Social Psychology*, *53*(4), 712-717. PDF: https://www. paulekman.com/wp-content/uploads/2013/07/Universals-And-Cultural-Differences-In-The-Judgment-Of-Facia.pdf

2. The Ekman Group, personal communication, July 22, 2015.

3. The Office of His Holiness The Dalai Lama. (2015, July 5). *Map of emotions and meditation on compassion*. Retrieved from http://www.dalailama.com/news/post/1293-map-of-emotions-and-meditation-on-compassion

4. Beck, J. (2014, February). New research says there are only four emotions. *The Atlantic Monthly*. Retrieved from http://www. theatlantic.com/health/archive/2014/02/new-research-says-there-are-only-four-emotions/283560/

    Jack, R., Garrod, O. G., & Schyns, P. G. (2014). Dynamic facial expressions of emotion transmit an evolving hierarchy of signals over time. *Current Biology*, 24, 187–192.

5. Jack, R., Garrod, O. G., & Schyns, P. G. (2014, January 2). Dynamic facial expressions of emotion transmit an evolving hierarchy of signals over time. Retrieved from https://www.youtube.com/watch?v=HNWMO7GkgOk

6. Ibid

7. Dossey, L. (2006). *The extraordinary healing power of ordinary things*. New York: Random House, 64-66.

8. Pert, C. (2004). Your body is your subconscious mind: New insights into the body-mind connection. Louisville, Colorado: Sounds True.

9. *10 questions for the Dalai Lama - Time Magazine interview*. (2010, June 14). Retrieved from His Holiness The 14th Dalai Lama of Tibet http://www.dalailama.com/messages/transcripts/10-questions-time-magazine

10. LeDoux, J. (2010). *Joseph LeDoux's biggest discoveries*. Retrieved from http://bigthink.com/videos/joseph-ledouxs-biggest-discoveries

11. Ibid

12. Solomon, G. J. (2006). *The heads-up on sports concussion*. Human Kinetics, 14.

13. Pert, C. (2004). Your body is your subconscious mind: New insights into the body-mind connection. Louisville, Colorado: Sounds True.

14. Tenzin Gyatso; The Fourteenth Dalai Lama. (n.d.). *Compassion and the individual*. Retrieved from http://www.dalailama.com/messages/compassion

15. Dossey, L. (1993). *Healing words*. New York, NY: Harper Collins, 19.

16. Ibid

17. Seligman, M. (1990). *Learned optimism.* New York, NY: Random House, 15-16.

18. Abraham Maslow: 1908-1970. (1998). In *WTTW 11.* Retrieved from http://www.pbs.org/wgbh/aso/databank/entries/bhmasl.html

19. Sousa, D. (2011). *How the brain learns* (4th ed.). Thousand Oaks, CA: Corwin, 69.

II. Eight Principles for Crafting Effective Mantras, Affirmations, and Autosuggestions

1. Patanjali. (2012). *The yoga sutras of Patanjali* (Revised Edition). (S. Satchidananda, Ed., & S. Satchidananda, Trans.) Yogaville, VA: Integral Yoga® Publications, p. 10.

2. CBS News. (2013, September 3). *Diana Nyad on epic swim: My mantra was "find a way".* Retrieved from http://www.cbsnews.com/news/diana-nyad-on-epic-swim-my-mantra-was-find-a-way/

3. Coué, E. (1922). *Self-Mastery through autosuggestion.* Retrieved from http://www.mind-your-reality.com/support-files/self_mastery_auto-suggestion_coue.pdf

4. Ahmed, S. H., Vandaelea, Y., & Guillema, K. (2013). Sugar addiction: Pushing the drug-sugar analogy to the limit. *Current Opinion in Clinical Nutrition and Metabolic Care, 16,* 434-439. doi: 10.1097/MCO.0b013e328361c8b8

5. Wong, H. (2009). *First days of school: How to be an effective teacher.* Mountain View, CA: Harry K. Wong Publications.

III. Hypnosis: Fact and Fiction

1. Spiegel, H. (2007). The neural trance: A new look at hypnosis. *International Journal of Clinical and Experimental Hypnosis, 55*(4), 387-410. doi: 10.1080/00207140701506367

2. Elkins, G. R. Barabasz, A.F., Council, J.R., & Spiegel, D. (2015). Advancing research and practice: The revised APA division 30 definition of hypnosis. *International Journal of Clinical and Experimental Hypnosis, 63*(1), 1-9. doi: 10.1080/00207144.2014.961870

3. Ibid

4. Kosslyn, S. M., Thompson, W. L., Costantini-Ferrando, M. F., Alpert, N. M., & and Spiegel, D. (2000). Hypnotic visual illusion alters color processing in the brain. *American Journal of Psychiatry*, *157* (8), 1279-1284. http://dx.doi.org/10.1176/appi.ajp.157.8.1279

5. Ibid

6. Spiegel, H. (2007). The neural trance: A new look at hypnosis. *International Journal of Clinical and Experimental Hypnosis, 55* (4), 387-410. doi: 10.1080/00207140701506367

7. Meyer, M., Raikes, J. (Producers), & Blumer, R. H. (Writer). (2006). *The new medicine* [Motion Picture].

8. theorgeorgio. (2011, June 11.) *Ellen stops smoking with hypnotherapy.* Retrieved from https://www.youtube.com/watch?v=KAPusbaf9KA.

    Allen Carr's Easyway Cyprus. (2010, February 27.) *Ellen DeGeneres stops smoking with Allen Carr's Easyway Method.* Retrieved from https://www.youtube.com/watch?v=Y9S4ojJRP2I

IV. Ten Steps to Relaxation and Self-Hypnosis

1. Spiegel, H. (1972). An eye-roll test for hypnotizability. *The American Journal of Clinical Hypnosis, 15* (1).

2. Ibid

Author's Request

Dear Reader,
As an author and researcher, I like feedback. I hear from my clients about how golden words and trance impacts them in our sessions together. I would also appreciate hearing from readers who would be willing to share their experiences.

HERE ARE SOME QUESTIONS FOR YOU TO THINK ABOUT:

What is a golden word to you?

What do golden words *feel* like to you?

How have you used golden words and tools to make positive life changes?

How have you used golden words and tools to overcome challenges?

In what way were the tools in this book useful to you?

In what way did you adapt any of these tools to fit your needs?

If you have children, how have you used golden words and tools with them?

What kinds of tools would you like to see in my forthcoming book *Golden Words for Kids?*

You can write to me at goldenwords@drsallystone.com to share your experiences. You can visit me on the web at www.DrSallyStone.com to learn more about my hypnosis and health coaching services, find my workshop schedule, read blog postings, and look for new publications.

Thank you,
Sally Stone